DURHAM EXECUTIONS
THE TWENTIETH CENTURY

By the same author
Foul Deeds and Suspicious Deaths in and Around Newcastle
Foul Deeds and Suspicious Deaths in and Around Durham
Foul Deeds and Suspicious Deaths Around the Tees
Executions and Hangings in Newcastle and Morpeth
Bygone Seaton Carew
Shipwrecks from the Tees to the Tyne
Durham Executions from 1700 to 1900

DURHAM EXECUTIONS

THE TWENTIETH CENTURY

MAUREEN ANDERSON

Wharncliffe Books

First Published in Great Britain in 2007 by
Wharncliffe Books
an imprint of
Pen and Sword Books Ltd
47 Church Street
Barnsley
South Yorkshire
S70 2AS

© Maureen Anderson 2007

ISBN: 978-1-84563–054-6

Typeset in 11/13pt Plantin by Concept, Huddersfield.

Printed and bound in England by
Antony Rowe Ltd, Chippenham, Wiltshire

Pen and Sword Books Ltd incorporates the Imprints of
Pen & Sword Aviation, Pen & Sword Maritime,
Pen & Sword Military, Wharncliffe Books,
Pen & Sword Select, Pen and Sword Military Classics
and Leo Cooper.

For a complete list of Pen & Sword titles please contact
PEN & SWORD BOOKS LIMITED
47 Church Street
Barnsley
South Yorkshire
S70 2AR
England
E-mail: enquiries@pen-and-sword.co.uk
Website: www.pen-and-sword.co.uk

Contents

Introduction

Prior to the nineteenth century, about 220 crimes were considered capital offences. Some of these included burglary, sacrilege, writing threatening letters, being in the company of gypsies for one month, adopting a disguise, stealing a handkerchief, shooting a rabbit (poaching) and forgery. Such offences could incur severe punishment: a prison sentence with hard labour, flogging and transportation (when that became an option). About twenty-five of those that were considered the more serious of these capital offences could see the perpetrator facing the end of a rope. There was no form of appeal and the executions were carried out within days – on some occasions only hours – of the death sentence being passed.

In 1861, the Criminal Law Consolidation Act came into being which allowed the death penalty to be limited to the crimes of murder, treason, arson and piracy with violence. Murder was the only crime in peacetime to be punishable by death. In these cases the law dictated that the courts had to impose the extreme penalty and the jury could only give a recommendation for mercy. It was then up to the prisoner and his defence to appeal to the Home Secretary and the eventually established Criminal Court of Appeal against the sentence.

In 1868, a law was passed against the practice of public executions. The gallows had to be erected within the prison walls and the execution witnessed only by the officials concerned. On most occasions the Press were still allowed to be present and a detailed (and often exaggerated) report would be published in the newspapers of the time. Allowing access to members of the Press was up to the justices and during a few executions at Durham in the nineteenth and early twentieth centuries this was denied.

The identity of the executioners who carried out some of the later executions remains unknown as the events were cloaked in secrecy to ensure the protection of the individuals concerned because of the strong public feeling against the death penalty.

The Homicide Act of 1957 brought about further changes to the law when diminished responsibility was reduced from a charge of murder to manslaughter. High treason and piracy remained unaffected and the crime of murder punishable by death was categorised into:

any murder done in the furtherance of theft; any murder by shooting or causing an explosion; any murder done in the course or for the purpose of resisting or avoiding or preventing a lawful arrest, or of affecting or assisting an escape or rescue from legal custody; any murder of a police officer acting in the execution of his duty or of a person assisting a prison officer so acting; two or more murders on different occasions.

This act caused utter confusion within the courts. It meant that if a person murdered someone while robbing them of a few pence the perpetrator could be hanged. If, however, a person planned a murder and carried it out by stabbing, poisoning or some other such method, but did not steal from their victim, they could escape the rope.

It was to be 1965 before the voices of the protestors against the death penalty were to be heeded and the protests acted upon. Britain abolished the death penalty for murder and in 2003 it was also abolished for piracy and high treason.

Although public sympathy is usually with the families of the murdered victims, and rightly so, one should perhaps also spare a thought for those nearest the person executed. Although not themselves the guilty party they would have to deal with the grief of losing their loved one and the stigma and guilt that a family member could take the life of another human being.

There is no doubt that a very small minority of those who breathed their last breath on a gibbet or a scaffold were innocent of the crime they had been accused of and were convicted on sparse, circumstantial evidence that would not hold up in court today.

Most of the condemned were of the lower working classes and, along with their families, may have been poor and only semi-literate with no possible means of arguing against the systems that were in place.

Year by year forensic science has taken mighty leaps forward and, if the death penalty was still an option of punishment in Britain, it would be highly improbable in the present day that an innocent person would be executed.

I would like to acknowledge and thank the following for their valued assistance in the compilation of this book: Maurice Henderson for information relating to his ancestors; Alf Carney for access to his wonderful collection of postcards; Michelle Russell for her artistic talents; the staff of Hartlepool Reference Library and Stephen White of the Carlisle Reference Library for their courtesy and willingness to seek out data; the team at Wharncliffe Books and Brian Elliott, Series Editor for making this publication possible and, last but not least, my husband, Jim for his never ending patience and support.

CHAPTER 1

Executioners

Many traditions and trades are carried on by succeeding generations but to have the office of executioner passed on through a family would seem to most of us quite bizarre. But, bizarre or not, there were two such families in Britain: Billington and Pierrepoint. James Billington was born in 1847 in Market Street, Farnworth, near Bolton and from an early age had been fascinated by executions. After employment as a wrestler, mill-hand and miner he took over the running of a barber's shop. During this time he unsuccessfully applied for William Marwood's hangman's job but instead, in 1894, he secured the position of hangman for Yorkshire. Eventually giving up his hairdressing business, he took over the running of the *Derby Arms* on Churchgate in Bolton whilst still carrying on with his part-time work as executioner.

Henry Pierrepoint often worked alongside Billington and the two were also great friends. Billington sent 147 people to their deaths before he succumbed to pneumonia and was taken by the Grim Reaper in December of 1901 at the age of fifty-four. Thomas Billington, born in

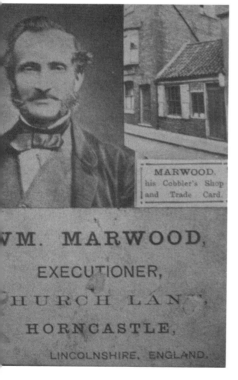

MARWOOD, his Cobbler's Shop and Trade Card.

VM. MARWOOD,

EXECUTIONER,

HURCH LANE,

HORNCASTLE,

LINCOLNSHIRE, ENGLAND.

This old postcard, published by WK Morton & Sons of Horncastle depicts William Marwood (in office 1875–83) and his cobbler's shop and trade card. On Marwood's retirement James Billington unsuccessfully applied to fill the position. Author's collection

1872, was James' oldest son and assisted his father on a few occasions. Always a sickly child, at the age of twenty-nine, he too contracted pneumonia and died in January 1902, just a month after his father. William, the next eldest son born in 1873, carried out executions from 1899 although he was not officially registered until 1900. He retired from the position in December 1903 and later spent time in prison for failing to maintain his wife and child. The longest surviving of the Billington boys, he died in 1934. The youngest, John, born in 1880, was also officially registered in 1900 assisting William on a number of occasions and carrying out sixteen executions as principal. John's career ended abruptly when he became ill with dropsy, dying at the age of twenty-five in 1905, leaving behind a wife and young child.

James Billington (1847–1901) held office as executioner 1884–1901. Author's collection

John Ellis was born in 1874 at Rochdale into a reasonably well-off family of hairdressers. He did not want to be part of the family business so at first he tried manual work but an injury to his back caused him to seek something less strenuous. Eventually, because his choices of work were limited, he opened a barber's shop in Oldham Road in Rochdale. Somewhere along the way the idea of becoming an executioner came into his mind. He wrote to the governor of Strangeways and was given an interview, training and, ultimately, a job.

John Ellis (1874–1932) held office as an executioner from 1901–24. Author's collection

Rochdale in Lancashire, where John Ellis was born in 1874. Author's collection

The pay at that time was £10 per execution for the principal and £2.10s (£2.50p) for an assistant. Ellis held the office of executioner from 1901 until March 1924 when he resigned due to poor health. In all he hanged 203 people including Dr Crippen at Pentonville Gaol for the murder of his wife and George Smith at Maidstone Gaol, who was responsible for the Brides in the Bath murders. In January 1923, assisted by Robert Baxter and Thomas Phillips, Ellis hanged Edith Thompson, who was convicted of being an accessory to the murder of her husband. Her execution took place at Holloway Gaol and she was so distressed that she had to be carried to the gallows. Ellis and William Willis also hanged Susan Newell at Glasgow, the second woman for Ellis in just nine months. Four months later Ellis gave in his notice as executioner. It was known that he disliked hanging women and it is probable that was why he gave up his post, although he told a newspaper journalist that was not the reason and that his worst day as an executioner was when he had to hang six men in Ireland, all before breakfast!

After his retirement Ellis wrote his memoirs which were published as a book, *Diary of a Hangman*. Alcohol became a real problem to Ellis and during one of his drinking bouts in 1924 he tried to shoot himself. He ended up in court charged with attempted suicide, which was, at the time, a criminal offence. He was bound over for twelve months and it was suggested by the court that he stay away from alcohol.

In December 1927, Ellis acted as the executioner William Marwood in the play *The Adventures of Charles Peace* but his acting career was short lived as the play was considered in such bad taste that it closed after a week. Ellis had kept his hairdressing business but in the 1930s the economy was bleak and the shop was not paying its way. He then took to the road giving demonstrations on executions. While working in London he became ill and had to return home. In 1932 Ellis had a particularly heavy drinking binge. He brandished a razor at his wife, Annie, and his daughter, Amy, threatening to cut their heads off. Austin Ellis, the eldest son, lived nearby and the two terrified women ran to his house for assistance. Austin immediately went to his parents' house but as he approached, his father was at the front door in the act of cutting his own throat. This time his suicide attempt was successful and he died on 20 September 1932 at the age of fifty-eight.

William Willis was from Accrington, Lancashire. Between 1906 and 1926 he acted as an assistant at more than 100 executions, working with John Ellis, Robert Baxter and Henry and Thomas Pierrepoint. Willis died in 1939.

George Brown acted as assistant at twenty executions between 1911 and 1919. Robert Wilson from Manchester also assisted Thomas Pierrepoint and was in office from 1920–36. Robert Baxter was born in Hertford and was in office from 1915–35.

Thomas Pierrepoint was born in 1870 and his brother, Henry, in 1874 at Clayton near Bradford. Henry's son, Albert, was born in 1905 and these three were the second family to follow the trade of hangmen. Henry was in office from 1901, when he acted as assistant to James Billington, and in total he carried out 107 executions throughout his career which ended in July 1910. Much later it came to light that Henry was sacked for arriving to perform an execution 'considerably the worse for drink' and for getting into a fight with John Ellis the previous day. Thomas was six years older than Henry and was in office from 1906 to 1946 retiring when he was in his mid-seventies. It is

Henry Pierrepoint (1874–1922) held office from 1901–10 and performed 107 executions within this period. Author's collection

thought he carried out about 300 executions. Thomas and Henry had both worked as assistants with Ellis and said after his suicide that he should have done it earlier as he was impossible to work with as he had paid far too much attention to detail. Thomas Mather Phillips assisted Thomas Pierrepoint from 1918 before he became a chief executioner until his retirement in 1941.

Albert Pierrepoint was in office from 1932 to 1956 and hanged an estimated 450 people including seventeen women. As well as in Britain, Albert also plied his trade in Germany executing war criminals.

Albert Pierrepoint (1905–92) held office from 1932–56 and executed 433 men and seventeen women within this period. Author's collection

One of his executions, along with his assistant, Syd Dernley, was Timothy John Evans on 9 March 1950 at Pentonville Gaol, who was convicted of murdering his wife at 10 Rillington Place. This was a case that is still remembered as a travesty of justice. John Reginald Halliday Christie was later convicted of the murder and admitted to killing another six women besides. Evans was granted a posthumous pardon in 1966. In 1951 Albert was credited with the fastest hanging on record when James Inglis was pronounced dead only seven seconds after leaving the cell. Albert's resignation was over a disagreement about his fee. He had arrived at Strangeways to perform an execution to find that there had been a reprieve. He should have received £15 but was only paid £1. Eventually he was paid another £4. Albert died in 1992 leaving behind an invaluable record in the form of his autobiography which was published in 1974. In this he writes:

It is I who have faced them last, young lads and girls, working men and grandmothers. It did not deter them then and it had not deterred them when they committed what they were convicted for. The fruit of my experience has this bitter after-taste: that I do not now believe that any one of the hundreds of executions I carried out has in any way acted as a deterrent against future murder. Capital punishment, in my view, achieved nothing except revenge.

Following the resignation of Albert Pierrepoint, Steve Wade and Harry Allen became joint chief executioners. Wade was from Doncaster and worked as an assistant to Thomas and Albert Pierrepoint at thirty-one executions from 1941. He carried out twenty-eight executions

Harry Bertrum Allen (1911–92) held office as executioner from 1941–64. Author's collection

as chief executioner with the last in August 1955 just a year before his death. Harry Bertrum Allen was born in Manchester in 1911 and was in office from 1941–64. He worked as assistant at about forty executions and as chief executioner he performed twenty-nine executions working in Cyprus as well as Britain. Allen executed Gwynne Owen Evans at Strangeways in August 1964 while at the same time Evan's accomplice, Peter Anthony Allen, was being hanged at Walton by Robert Leslie Stewart. These were the last two men to be hanged in Britain. Stewart died in 1988 and Allen in 1992. Robert Stewart was from Edinburgh and acted as assistant and officiated in twenty-six executions from 1950–64.

Others that were on the Home Office list and, besides other counties, were involved in the carrying out of executions at Durham were Harry Kirk from Huntingdon who assisted at about thirty-five executions and acted as principal at only one throughout his period, from 1941–50. Thomas Cuncliffe assisted at four executions from 1958–9.

Syd Dernley was born in Mansfield, Nottingham in 1920. On leaving school at the age of fifteen he went to work at Sherwood

Colliery. From the age of eleven he had been interested in crime and his wish was to become a hangman. He wrote that it was not because he wished to kill people but because he wanted to travel and meet notorious criminals and famous detectives. He applied for a post as an executioner in 1947 but it was to be some time before he was accepted. Eventually he took his training and performed his first execution in 1949 at Durham Gaol and his last in December of 1952. Although he was never chief executioner, he assisted at twenty-five hangings throughout his career. Dernley and his wife, Joyce, then took over a post

Syd Dernley (1920–94) held office as assistant executioner from 1949 and performed his last execution in 1952.
Author's collection

office until their retirement. After a programme on radio about capital punishment, along with David Newman, who worked for the radio station, Dernley produced a book on his memoirs which was published as *The Hangman's Tale*. He died in 1994, the last in a long line of British hangmen.

CHAPTER 2

Durham Gaol

To replace the old gaol in the great North Gate, the building of the present Durham Gaol at Elvet began with the foundation stone being laid on 31 July 1809 by Sir Henry Vane Tempest. The sum of £2,000 was pledged towards the cost by Bishop Shute Barrington, last but one of the Prince Bishops, who ruled from 1791 to 1826. The first architect was sacked, the second died, the building eventually being completed by Ignatius Bonomi. The first prisoners were incarcerated within its walls in 1819.

Until 1816 executions took place at Dryburn, probably at a spot within the grounds of the present Dryburn Hospital. The name Dryburn (or dry stream) is said to stem from a time when a Jesuit priest was executed at the spot where a water course once flowed. After the priest's death the stream dried up never to flow again. The place of execution was moved in 1816 to the steps outside the courthouse where a temporary gallows was erected for each hanging.

Between 1800 and 1899 forty-five people were hanged at Durham, three of them women. The last public execution was carried out by Thomas Askern on 16 March 1865 on Matthew Atkinson for beating his wife to death at Winlaton. For private executions, a gallows was set up inside one of the prison yards and all that could be seen by the public was the black flag being hoisted and a notice pinned to the gates or the doors reporting that the felon was dead. In the twentieth century, Durham was one of a few British gaols to erect a permanent structure. This was situated on the ground floor of one of the wings with the trap falling open to the basement.

At Newcastle Gaol the last execution took place in November 1919, with the prison finally closed down on 31 March 1925. Although trials still took place at Newcastle for crimes within

Durham Old Gaol, which was on the Great North Gate, was replaced with the present buildings in 1810. Author's collection

that area, those condemned to death were transported to Durham Gaol for execution.

Between 1900 and 1958 there were a total of fifty-five men hanged at Durham Gaol, all being convicted of murder, the last execution taking place on Wednesday 17 December 1958.

Newcastle Gaol where the last execution took place in November 1919. Following the closure of the gaol in 1925 those sentenced to death at Newcastle Assizes were executed at Durham Gaol. Author's collection

Durham Assizes, built in 1810, was where many of the convicted felons were sentenced to death. The author

CHAPTER 3

The Sea-Coal Gatherer 1900

Isabella Bowes was known to be a hard-working woman, having eked out a living for her family for many years. Not so fifty-year old John, her husband, who was a bricklayer by trade but declined to go out to work. In 1900, the couple lived with their twenty-one-year-old daughter at Seaham Harbour. Isabella spent her days on the beach collecting sea-coal and then selling it. Most of her income appeared to be used to keep her husband in alcohol as he was often drunk. When in drink Bowes would become abusive and violent, constantly hurling jealous accusations at his wife.

On Tuesday 21 August 1900, there was a particularly nasty episode when Bowes had torn up some of his daughter's clothes and threatened to kill both her and his wife. In fear of their lives

The village of Seaham Harbour, the home of John and Isabella Bowes.
Author's collection

the two women left the house and went to stay with friends. Isabella decided she had had enough and was not going to return to her husband so applied for a separation order and took out a summons against him.

On Saturday 8 September, Isabella went to the beach as usual and, as she picked up coal near to the ballast tips, her husband approached her. There were a number of people on the beach at the time, including Isabella's daughter, Edith Cook, Anne Jane Wright and a young boy, Proctor, who all witnessed the events that followed. The couple argued for a few minutes and then Isabella turned her back on her husband and bent down to pick up a lump of coal. As she did so Bowes snatched up a heavy piece of wood and, with great force, hit his wife on the back of her head. Isabella fell to the ground and Bowes struck her a further three times before throwing the wood to one side and marching off a few paces down the beach towards the sea. He then took a rag from his pocket, wet it with sea water and, returning to his wife, sat on the beach and lifted her head onto his lap and began bathing her face. By this time one of the witnesses had gone to fetch the police.

When PC Fearne arrived at the scene Bowes was still cradling his wife's head and crying that he loved her. Isabella was taken to Seaham Harbour infirmary where she died a few hours later without regaining consciousness.

Bowes stood trial at Durham on Saturday 24 November before Justice William Grantham with Mr Luck and Mr Meek for the prosecution and Edward Shortt for the defence. Bowes admitted his guilt and said he deserved to die for his actions. The jury took just five minutes to bring in a verdict of guilty. The death sentence was passed and as Bowes left the dock he bowed to the judge.

As Bowes awaited his execution he was visited by friends and family including the daughter that had given testimony against him. The only mention he made of his act was to say that he would rather hang than spend the rest of his days in penal servitude. By 7.30 am, on Wednesday 12 December 1900, a large crowd had gathered outside the gaol.

There was a winter sun struggling through the clouds making it like a spring morning when Bowes, looking pale and haggard,

The beach at Seaham where Isabella Bowes was murdered by her husband in 1900.
Author's collection

was led to the scaffold. As a result of alcohol and jealousy he paid the ultimate price when he was hanged by James and William Billington.

This was not the first time that Seaham beach had been the locality for a brutal killing. On 2 August 1889, eight-year-old Caroline Winter had been found raped and murdered and left in a pool of water to appear as if she had drowned. The body of a man found washed to shore about ten days later was thought to have been that of the perpetrator. It was believed that the unidentified man saw no escape from punishment for his crime so had committed suicide. This, however, was never proved so officially Caroline's murder remains unsolved to this day.

CHAPTER 4

A Defence of Insanity
1901

Mary Ann was married to Lazare Lieutand at Newcastle in 1896. Employed as a ship's steward, Lieutand was often away from home on long sea voyages and eventually Mary, or Maggie as she was known, became fed up with the loneliness while her husband was away and the arguing when he was at home. In 1901, when she was thirty-three, the couple separated and Maggie met and entered into a relationship with John George Thompson, setting up home with him at Byker. Thompson was thirty-nine and had been employed as an engine fitter at Armstrong's works for about seven years. The relationship did not turn out to be a happy one and Maggie ended the affair and went to live with her friend, Ivy Dawson, at 121 Milling Street in Gateshead. The accommodation was an upper flat comprising of four rooms which was reached by a small staircase from a passage that ran from the front to back on the ground floor of the house.

On Friday 13 September, about four weeks after Maggie had moved to Milling Street, Thompson turned up at the door. Maggie, although nervous, invited him in and introduced him to Ivy. Thompson wanted to speak to Maggie alone but she refused saying he would have to leave as she and Ivy were going to Newcastle for the day. He appeared very annoyed but left and the two women went on their trip. That evening in Newcastle they came upon Thompson in Grainger Street and afterwards spotted him several times and realised that he was following them. They were quite frightened by this and, to be amongst people, stayed in Newcastle as late as possible. When they were returning home at about midnight they watched their house for a few minutes from the end of their street to make sure Thompson was not there.

On the following Monday morning, Maggie and Ivy went into the Askew Road post office to mail some letters. When they came out Thompson was waiting for them and once again asked Maggie if she would speak to him. She told him she had nothing to discuss and Ivy told him he should leave her alone. He became very angry and threatening before storming off. The two friends then went to visit Maggie's sister and as they returned on a tram saw Thompson walking towards their house. Instead of getting off the tram at their usual stop they stayed aboard and alighted two stops further on. They then walked back towards the house, intending to approach it from the rear entrance but Thompson had seen them and as the two women hurried along the street he followed close behind shouting to Maggie. Ivy unlocked the door and pushed Maggie into the passage and then followed her but before she could lock their pursuer out he had wedged his foot in the door forcing it open. As Maggie stood and faced him he pulled a revolver from his right hand pocket and fired. She screamed as the bullet caught her shoulder. On the opposite side of the road the door of 122 had opened as the occupant, Mrs Boyle, had come out to see what the disturbance was. Ivy shouted to Maggie to run over there. As Maggie entered, Mrs Boyle tried to close the door but Thompson managed to hold it slightly open with his foot while at the same time putting his arm through the gap and firing the revolver twice. Although he could not see who or what he was aiming at, Maggie was in the line of fire and one bullet hit her in the arm and the other lodged in her head. Ivy had sent for the police and when Sergeant William Cockburn of Gateshead arrived on the scene Thompson was sitting on the floor holding the unconscious woman's hand. He freely admitted that the shooting was his doing and gave the revolver up willingly. Cockburn instructed a neighbour to stay with the victim while he took Thompson to lock him up and send for a doctor. Maggie was taken to her house but died soon after without regaining consciousness.

The trial was held at Durham Assizes on Saturday 23 November before Justice William Grantham with Mr Luck and Ralph Simey for the prosecution and Edward Shortt for the defence. Thompson admitted his guilt but in his defence put

A sketch by Robert Bertram of Blackett Street in Newcastle. It was here that John Thompson purchased the revolver which he used to shoot and kill Maggie Lieutand in 1901. Author's collection

forward a plea of temporary insanity. Medical evidence from Dr Steele of Durham County Asylum disputed Thompson's defence saying he could find no evidence whatsoever to support the claim. It was established that on the morning of the murder Thompson had bought the revolver from a shop in Blackett Street in Newcastle and then a box of cartridges from another shop. The jury were unanimous in deciding that this was not an act of momentary insanity but a deliberate premeditated act and they brought in a verdict of guilty of wilful murder.

On Tuesday 10 December, after a frosty night, the morning dawned bright and clear. In a procession comprised of the prison governor, the under sheriff, three warders, a surgeon and the prison chaplain, Thompson was escorted to the scaffold. Although deathly pale, he walked with a military step to take his place on the drop. The chief executioner, William Billington, placed the hood over Thompson's head while his brother, Thomas, assisted by adjusting the ankle strap. There was little for the crowd of a hundred or so people that had gathered outside the walls to see. As the cathedral clock rang out its eighth chime a buzzer sounded and the black flag was hoisted signifying that the execution had been completed.

CHAPTER 5

Three Generations
1902

Justice J Channell had to find justice for four victims when the cases of two men accused of murder were heard before him at the Durham Assizes in November of 1902. The first of the cases was that of Samuel Walton who was accused of three murders, that of his baby daughter, wife and mother-in-law. His trial was heard on Monday 24 November with Hans Hamilton acting for the prosecution and F Mortimer for the defence.

Samuel and Isabella Walton lived at Spennymoor in a not too happy marriage. They had separated at one time but had decided to get back together and try again. On 23 August 1902,

St Paul's church at Spennymoor. The author

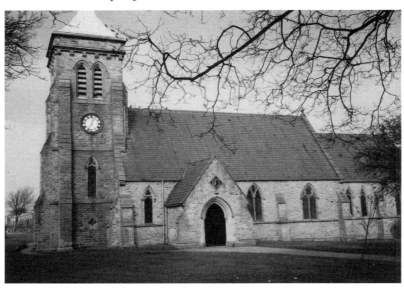

nine years into the marriage, the couple had a really heated argument which resulted in Walton throwing his wife out into the street but keeping their eleven-month-old daughter, Esther Jane, with him. Isabella went to her mother, Isabella Young, at Middlestone Moor and the two women went to the police to ask them to get the baby out of the house. PC Lambert went to the house with them and Walton allowed them to enter to get the baby, then ordered them all out. When Lambert warned Walton about his conduct he replied that he would shoot them all and then give himself up to the police.

Mrs Young took her daughter and granddaughter to stay with her and, after some soul searching; Isabella decided enough was enough and that the marriage should end. She took legal advice and acquired a separation order and custody of her daughter. Walton, who worked as a miner, was instructed to pay maintenance of 10s (50p) a week beginning on 11 September but he had other ideas. On 9 September, Walton sold all the household furniture and went to stay with a friend, Arthur Edmund Crow. On the following day, Walton and Crow visited the *Commercial Hotel* at Tudhoe Grange. There was a pawnshop next door where Walton purchased a Belgium Bulldog revolver and fifty cartridges for 10s 6d. He showed it to some friends saying that he would pay his 10s with that. Perhaps his friends thought he was bluffing because they told him that he was being foolish but no one thought to inform the police or the family of Walton's threats.

On Thursday 10 September, the day the payment was due, Walton went to Isabella's mother's house. When his mother-in-law, Mrs Young, answered the door he told her he had come to pay the maintenance but he wanted a receipt. She turned away from the door, presumably to fetch paper and pen, and as she did so Walton shot her. He then entered the house and shot both his wife and daughter before cutting his own throat with a gully knife. Although Isabella was in a serous condition she managed to run from the house and alert neighbours.

Dr RS Anderson of Spennymoor and the police arrived at the house to find Mrs Young dead and Walton lying on the bed cradling his dying child. Isabella was taken to Bishop Auckland Cottage Hospital where she died on Thursday 18 September.

Durham infirmary where Samuel Walton was taken to be treated after an attempt to cut his own throat. Author's collection

She had suffered a gunshot wounds to one of her hands as she had raised it to defend herself and a bullet had passed through her head and out of the other side. Walton was taken to Durham infirmary where his wound was found not to be life threatening.

An initial inquest was held at the *Binchester Hotel* into the charge against Walton of the murder of his daughter and Isabella Young, his mother-in-law. When his wife succumbed to her injuries the charges of murder became three and Walton was committed to stand trial at Durham Assizes. It was clear that the murders had been premeditated as Walton had made no secret of the fact that he had purchased a revolver with that intention. The defence put forward a case showing that Walton had been a good workman, husband and father until his world was turned upside down by the departure of his wife and the child he doted on. He then became a totally different character, becoming full of rage. The prosecution pointed out that it was not the court's place to decide who was at fault in the break-down of the marriage. After all the evidence had been heard the jury, without leaving their box, returned a verdict of guilty of the wilful murder of three generations of women and for this Walton received sentence of death. As Walton left the dock he was smiling.

Isabella Young, who was fifty-three, and Esther Walton were buried in Binchester churchyard on Sunday 15 September. The road from the Young's house to the churchyard was lined with people wanting to say farewell to their popular neighbour and her small granddaughter. Isabella Walton was buried alongside them a few days later.

Brutal Attack of an Innocent, 1902

James Stewart, a brick-maker, lived at 16 Joel Terrace, Bill Quay. Stewart was a widower and the father of six children one of whom was seven-year-old Mary Ina. On the morning of Saturday 16 August Stewart had gone to work at Hexham and Mary and her friend, Joanna Geraldine Scott, who was eleven, went to visit Mary's Uncle Frederick at 8 Gosforth Terrace, Pelaw which was a short distance away over a bank known as Hilly Fields. Stewart returned home at about 10.30 pm to find that Mary was not at home and thinking she must still be at his brother's house he set off to collect her. When he arrived at Gosforth Terrace he was told that his brother had watched Mary set off over Hilly Fields at about 7.30 pm. Stewart questioned Joanna who told him that she had not seen Mary since they had parted company just after they left Frederick's

The town of Hexham where James Stewart had been working on the day his daughter was murdered. Author's collection

house. Joanna lived at Heworth so the two girls took different routes to reach their homes. Mary's father, by now extremely alarmed, called on friends and neighbours to organise search parties to look for his daughter. Willing participants combed the area all through that night and the following day. One of the first places to be searched was Wood, Skinner and Company's disused brickyard but because of the long grass that covered the site it was decided on Monday that something could have been missed so the area should be searched again. One of the searchers, William Taylor, eventually made the grim discovery, finding the little girl's body beside a wooden wall and covered with long grass. An examination of the body by Dr JW Mackey of Pelaw revealed that the cause of death had been asphyxiation combined with shock. That the little girl had been murdered was tragedy enough but when the nature of the injuries she had suffered was disclosed everyone in the vicinity was horrified. There were marks to her throat and to her nostrils. It appeared a hand had been held over her mouth to stop her from screaming and she had either choked on her own blood or been throttled to death. Multiple wounds to her head and arms had been inflicted with a blunt instrument. Mary had also been violently sexually assaulted and some sort of implement, probably a knife, had been used on her lower body to allow penetration of the male organ. Further injuries had then been caused by this act and there would have been considerable loss of blood. The medical examiner thought that the child was probably unconscious or already dead when the worst injury was inflicted.

Mary was buried at Heworth cemetery on Thursday 21 August where Rev Dr Steel preached his sermon to a large gathering of people. Many of the mourners had not known the family but were still deeply affected by the nature of the child's death.

This was a case that caused such public outrage that it had to be solved very quickly and the police lost no time in starting enquiries which led them to arrest Thomas Nicholson. He was twenty-three, lived at Back Ann Street in Bill Quay with his mother and worked as a cart-man for Robert Davidson at Woodgate Farm.

A view of Bill Quay near Gateshead where Mary Ina Stewart was brutally raped and murdered by Thomas Nicholson in 1902. Author's collection

Initial trials were held at the Wesleyan School in Bill Quay where the first to give evidence was William F Stock, the County Analyst. He had found spots of blood on Nicholson's trousers and coat but could not say whether they were fresh; there was no trace of semen. Nicholson's pocket knife had also been examined and found to have blood upon it but, again, there was no way of knowing how long it had been there. It had been raining heavily before the body was found so because the child's clothes were saturated with water very little could be determined from them except for a few bloodstains. After further inquests and the testimony of numerous witnesses it was decided there was enough evidence against Nicholson to commit him for trial.

At Durham Assizes, on Wednesday 26 November 1902, before Justice Channell with J Edmondson Joel and EA Mitchell-Innes for the Crown and Ralph Simey for the defence Nicholson stood accused of wilful murder with the events of the fateful evening slowly revealed.

Nicholson had been with James Dinning on the Saturday with another man at the *Wardley Hotel* and then later the *Mason's Arms* at Felling Shore. The two men had parted company at about 6.30 pm with Nicholson being a little worse for wear. A short time after this, Thomas Hedley Douglas, a twelve-year-old boy, had seen Nicholson walking backwards and forwards on Hilly Fields. Another witness, Alice Nichols, had seen a man talking to Mary and then walking with her holding her hand. She thought, by the man's demeanour, that he was drunk. At a later line-up she was unable to identify Nicholson as the man she had seen. Although other witnesses put the accused man in the vicinity no one had seen him in the company of the little girl.

When Nicholson was arrested the suit he had been wearing on the day of the murder had been pawned by his mother. This was not unusual as Mrs Nicholson had done this previously when she had been short of money. The suit was recovered by the police and passed to the County Analyst for examination. When Nicholson was asked to explain his movements around the time the little girl had disappeared he told the police that he had not left the pub until closing but numerous witnesses testified that he had left sometime around 6.30 pm and had not returned. He had also been seen at about 3 am on Sunday standing outside his front door looking extremely nervous.

Although all the evidence was circumstantial, Nicholson's version of events was full of contradictions and the jury took only a very short time to bring in a verdict of guilty. It took even less time for Justice Channell to give his summing up speech and to pass sentence of death.

On Tuesday 16 December 1902, Thomas Nicholson and Samuel Walton were pinioned and led towards the scaffold in

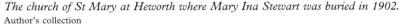

The church of St Mary at Heworth where Mary Ina Stewart was buried in 1902.
Author's collection

a procession headed by the chaplain reciting the opening sentences for the burial of the dead. As they passed the few members of the Press that had been admitted to the proceedings it was observed that both men appeared very haggard. As the two men stood side by side on the drop Walton turned to Nicholson and said: 'Good morning lad, keep thee heart up.' These were the last words spoken before William and John Billington had the ankle straps, hoods and ropes in place and the lever pulled which sent the two men to the hereafter.

CHAPTER 6

A Volatile Relationship 1903

Ellen Newman was married but this did not stop her having an affair with James Duffy, a shipyard worker. He was a widower living with his youngest child, a boy of fourteen, at Windsor Terrace in Grangetown. Ellen eventually left her husband and moved in with Duffy and it became common knowledge that the couple were known to enjoy more than a moderate drink. Duffy did not bother working as Ellen brought enough into the house earned by prostitution. The relationship was fraught with drunken, violent quarrels which sometimes ended in serious injury. In November 1902, Duffy had slashed Ellen's throat and then his own but they had both survived, with Duffy being imprisoned for a month for his actions. While he was in prison Ellen moved to 4 Back Durham Street. When Duffy was released they re-kindled the relationship and he moved in with her.

On Saturday 5 September 1903, Mrs Hope, who lodged with Ellen, arrived back at the house just after 11 pm to find Duffy asleep in a chair. He woke up in a foul mood and lashed out at his son who was in the room at the time. Mrs Hope had words with him about hitting the boy and Duffy said he was going to bed. At that point Ellen stormed out of the house shouting that she was not going to 'live with a pig like him' any longer. Duffy followed and managed to persuade her to return and the household finally quietened down.

At 1.45 the following morning Duffy walked into the central police station and said he was giving himself up for murder. The police went to the house to find Ellen's lifeless body on the bed.

Duffy stood trial at Durham Assizes on Saturday 21 November, before Justice William Grantham with Hans Hamilton and

Kevin H Marshall for the prosecution; and Mr Chadman for the defence. His version was that he had strangled Ellen in self-defence because, when they had gone to bed, they had begun to argue again and Ellen had threatened to hit him with a lamp. Duffy had grabbed her around the throat, not realising that his grip was firm enough to kill her. Although witnesses confirmed that Ellen had a violent temper, Duffy's plea of her death being an accident fell on deaf ears and the jury brought in a 'guilty of wilful murder' verdict. He was hanged on Tuesday 8 December 1903 by William and John Billington.

Justice William Grantham, the presiding judge at the trial of James Duffy in 1903. Author's collection

CHAPTER 7

For the Love of Margaret 1904

On the morning of Wednesday 6 July 1904, a man walked into the County Police Barracks at Durham and handed over a written confession to a murder. He was George Breeze, a twenty-one-year-old miner and a member of the Seaham White Star Football team. The woman he claimed to have murdered was twenty-year-old Margaret Jane Chisholm. Police Constable Trueman went to the house at 9 Back South Railway Street in Seaham where he found Margaret lying on the bed with her two-year-old child standing by her side and slapping her mother's hands trying to wake her. Margaret would never wake again as she had been strangled. On the kitchen was another written confession explaining what

The village of Seaham where George Breeze murdered Margaret Chisholm in 1904.
Author's collection

had taken place and that Breeze had gone to the police station to give himself up.

Margaret had been married for three years to Thomas Chisholm who worked as a miner at New Seaham Colliery. He had become friendly with Breeze at work and offered him lodgings at his house. It was not long before Breeze fell in love with Margaret and, he said, she with him. It would have been an impossible situation as the accommodation consisted of only one room and Breeze slept on the sofa in the same room as Margaret and her husband.

According to Breeze, on the fateful day Margaret had risen early and given her husband his breakfast before he left for work. When Breeze woke up soon after, Margaret told him that she and her husband had argued because he had become wise to what was happening. She added that she was desperately unhappy and wished she was dead. Breeze asked her if he should kill her and she had answered that she did not care. He had then strangled Margaret, written out the two confessions and made his way to the police station.

Breeze's trial was held at Durham on Saturday 16 July before Justice William Grantham with Hans Hamilton and Coutts Trotter for the prosecution. Mr Ball was appointed to act as defence but Breeze refused representation stating that he deserved to die for what he had done. The jury had no choice but to bring in a verdict of guilty. When His Lordship pronounced sentence of death Breeze said that he hoped there would be no reprieve as he wished to die so he could be with the woman he loved. His wish was granted when he was hanged on Tuesday 2 August 1904 by William Billington and John Ellis.

CHAPTER 8

To Catch a Thief
1908

Windy Nook had long been known for the quality grindstones that were produced from the local quarries but in 1907 the vicinity became famous for a completely different reason. Over a period of a month or so, there appeared to be evidence of theft at the local Co-operative store. In the butcher's shop on the corner of Union and Harwood Streets, meat that was thought to have been in the store at closing seemed to have vanished when the store re-opened but there was no sign of a break-in. An inventory was taken and it was found that small quantities of meat had indeed gone missing. Sawdust was sprinkled on the floor of the butcher's section to determine whether this was being imagined or if they did really have a burglar. The following morning there were footprints through the sawdust proving that there had been an intruder. For some obscure reason, with disastrous consequences, instead of informing the police, the managing committee drew up a rota of men to hide and keep watch within the store at night until the thief could be apprehended. On Thursday 31 October, it was the turn of John Patterson, George Ather, Christopher Carr and John Joseph Cowell to be night watchmen so they settled themselves in the butcher's section to wait. They had rigged up a device so that the dimmed lamp could be turned up quickly. Around 1 am they heard the local policeman, PC John James Thompson, checking the door as he did his rounds and then all was quiet.

Just as they must have been thinking that their watch was going to be uneventful, at about 4 am, the street light outside was extinguished and they heard the front door being unlocked and saw a shadowy figure, with what looked like a stick under his arm, enter the store. The watchmen waited until the intruder was close and leapt out at him. Cowell tried to turn up the light but nothing happened and what followed took place in semi-darkness. Although the watchers had the element of surprise their prey fought back hard. Carr picked up a butcher's steel and hit the man twice but he still fought on. Cowell then saw a gun in the man's hand and shouted a warning but it was too late. A shot rang out and caught Patterson in the head, killing him instantly. A second shot caught Carr in the leg and he fell to the floor. Ather and Cowell ran outside and began trying to fasten the door to trap the intruder inside but the man had stood on a barrel and was escaping through a side window. Cowell had handed Ather a hammer and he managed to strike the intruder on the leg before he disappeared into the night.

The police had quite a few clues to follow up. The killer had dropped a false beard, a hazel stick, with which it was thought he had sabotaged the streetlight, a cap and a lamp. The barrel that he had used to stand on to reach the window contained lard and this had left a clear imprint of his shoe when he jumped to the ground outside. The police also knew that the man would have been injured in the scuffle.

Suspicion fell on Joseph William Noble, a forty-eight-year-old family man who was employed at the North-Eastern Railway Company's Gateshead works. Noble was covered in bruises and said he had fallen at work whilst carrying some iron but had not reported the incident to his employers. This explanation did not satisfy the police as the injuries appeared to be more consistent with a beating than a fall and he was taken into custody. On a search being made of his house the police found hazel sticks matching the one left at the store and a number of items which had Co-operative store labels on them. The footprints in the lard matched his shoe and they also found gun cartridges and a set of keys. These were skeleton keys which had been fashioned to open any door, including those at the store. Noble was an extremely skilled blacksmith and would have easily been able to make the keys. Another factor in his demise was that although no gun was found, the cartridges matched those that had been fired at the crime scene. He was charged with murder and committed to stand trial.

Noble stood at Durham Assizes on Monday 2 March 1908 before Justice Channell with J Scott-Fox, Bruce Williamson and Walter Hedley for the prosecution and Morgan Griffiths-Jones and Edward Shortt for the defence. Although Noble denied being anywhere near the scene of the crime the circumstantial evidence was weighted against him although there were points which pointed to a possibility of innocence. The footprints made by the lard did not lead directly to Noble's house. The Co-operative's goods that were found could not be identified as having been stolen as they had not been missed. The cartridges were old and corroded and a gun was never found. Noble said that he had been given the skeleton keys by his father many years previously and that he had never owned a gun. The shots were fired by someone using his left hand but Noble claimed he was right-handed. This was disputed as it was stated that in his work he could use either hand with dexterity. Noble's defence had no sway on the jury as the chain of strong circumstantial evidence pointed solely to him and he was found guilty and sentenced to death.

The peaceful church of St Alban at Windy Nook. It was here John Patterson was buried in 1908. Author's collection

Although the community was appalled at the murder there were questions as to why the authorities had not been informed of the suspicion that Noble was stealing from the store rather than setting up a vigilante group. If the proper channels had been followed Noble could have been arrested for a lesser crime and two lives would not have needlessly been lost. John Patterson, buried at St Alban's Church, Windy Nook, left behind a widow and a twin boy and girl.

She was Leaving, 1908
Robert Lawman, a miner working at Elswick Colliery, was separated from his wife and two children and had been living with Amelia Bell Wood for a little over three years. When these events took place Lawman was thirty-five and Amelia twenty-four. The couple were heavy drinkers and rows were not uncommon as Amelia liked the high life rather than the drudgery of housekeeping. In January 1908, Amelia left Lawman and moved into new lodgings run by Elizabeth Senior at 1 Hyde Park Street in Gateshead. The next day, Lawman arrived at the lodgings and, after introducing himself to the landlady, gave her some money and asked her to get them some whisky and beer. Elizabeth bought the drink and Lawman took it into the room occupied by Amelia. The following morning, Saturday 1 February, Elizabeth began to prepare breakfast when she heard a moan coming from the couple's room. She knocked and tried the door but it was locked and there was no answer so she decided to leave them to their privacy and went back to the kitchen. A few minutes later there was a terrible scream. Still not able to gain access and, by now extremely alarmed, Elizabeth ran out of the house to alert the police. When PC Patrick Kelly returned with the landlady he tried to force the door but had to send Elizabeth for further assistance. Two more officers arrived and when the three policemen forced the door open it was to reveal Amelia's body lying in a pool of blood from a deep, jagged gash to her throat. Lawman's throat was also cut and he was taken to Gateshead Hospital. His wound was not severe and with medical attention he survived to stand trial.

The trial was held at Durham Assizes on Friday 28 February, before Justice Channell with CF Lowenthal and H Mundahi acting for the prosecution and Morgan Griffith Jones for the defence. Lawman said that he could not bear the thought of life without Amelia and his intention was for them both to die. The knife that had been used was shown to the jury. It had been sharpened to resemble a saw with serrated edges and Amelia would have died within seconds of it being drawn across her throat. If Lawman had used just a little more force on himself he would have also been dead. Perhaps Lawman's sad story may have swayed the jury towards a verdict of manslaughter but for the fact that one of Lawman's two children, William, testified as to his often violent behaviour towards their mother. His Lordship would not allow the youngest child, George, to give evidence. It was also established that Lawman was often violent when he had been drinking and had assaulted Amelia in the past. A verdict of guilty of wilful murder was brought and sentence of death was handed down.

The only hint as to what was to take place behind the forbidding walls of Durham Gaol at 9 am on Tuesday 24 March were two small notices pinned to the gates on the previous day:

Thomas and Henry Pierrepoint who hanged Robert Lawman in 1908.
Author's collection

The sentence of the law passed upon Joseph William Noble found guilty of murder will be carried into execution at 9 am tomorrow. Colonel Rowland Burdon, Sheriff of Durham. John Dillion, Governor of Durham Gaol.

The second notice was identical except for the substitution of the name Robert Lawman. Noble had written a last letter to his wife in which he swore to his innocence of the crime. Three members of the press were present as well as the usual officials and the executioners, Henry and Thomas Pierrepoint. As the cathedral clock chimed nine the condemned men were hanged side by side. The practice of raising a black flag was a thing of the past so the crowd of 200 or so that had gathered outside the gates saw nothing other than the notices being replaced with words to the effect that the deed was done.

The New Will, 1908
Mary Jane Marquis was a widow of means when she married forty-year-old Matthew James Dodds in 1905. Including the property she herself lived in she owned seven houses in the village of Hamsterley as well as having a healthy bank balance. Dodds, although partially crippled, was a master joiner so, presumably, would have been helpful in the maintenance of his wife's properties. The marriage did not turn out to be a happy one and there were constant arguments which were often heard by neighbours.

On Thursday 20 February 1908, shouting was heard to come from the Dodds' house but, as it was a regular occurrence, it was ignored. Dodds's version of events were that he had been working at his father's joinery shop until 4 pm and when he had arrived home it was to find his wife's body lying on the hearth of the fire badly burnt. He went for a neighbour, Sarah Wade, who, on entering the living room, saw Mary Jane with her clothes still smouldering and clutching a cinder in her hand. There was a shawl wrapped tight around the dead woman's neck but it was assumed that this had caught on the fender and become twisted. At the inquest into Mary's death an open verdict was recorded and her body was released to be buried at St James' Church on 23 February.

The village of Hamsterley where Mary Jane Dodds was murdered by her husband in 1908. Author's collection

The police had not been entirely convinced that Dodds had been telling the truth and when the rumours and innuendos that were being bandied about that Mary Jane's death was not accidental came to their ears they decided to carry out further enquiries. Once they had interviewed all the neighbours they decided there was enough evidence to arrest Dodds on suspicion of murder. Sixteen days after her death Mary Jane's body was exhumed for further medical examination. The resulting findings were that Mary had been strangled with her own shawl but it could not be ascertained whether the burns had been inflicted before or after death. Dodds was charged with her murder and at a hearing held at Bishop Auckland was found guilty and committed to trial.

Dodds stood at Durham Assizes on Wednesday 1 July 1908 before Justice William Grantham with CF Lowenthal and H Mundahl for the prosecution and Edward Shortt and S Fleming for the defence. The story of a murder for money gradually unravelled through both circumstantial and factual evidence. Mary Jane's initial will named her husband as the sole beneficiary but in 1907 she had changed this leaving him just a mere £40. Presumably she had done this because the relationship was so unhappy and perhaps she thought this may bring her husband to heel. Although a large sum at the time it would not have made Dodds a wealthy man nor would it make him the man of property that he must have visualised.

In January 1908 Dodds had copied out the first will and had somehow talked or brow-beaten Mary Jane into signing it. When she signed the document little did she know she was putting her name to her own death warrant. It will never be certain whether Dodds intended to kill his wife when he had her sign this final will or if the idea to give fate a helping hand to make him rich came afterwards, but fifty-year-old Mary Jane was dead a month later. Neighbours testified to seeing and hearing frequent quarrels between the couple and to Mary Jane often having cuts and bruises inflicted by Dodds. The landlady of the *Cross Keys*, Alice Stephenson, said Dodds was often violent towards his wife in her establishment and Mary Jane complained to her of his cruel treatment. On the day she died neighbours had heard her screaming but had not interfered because it was commonplace. Dodds's explanation of his bad treatment towards his wife was that she drank and this caused animosity between them.

The most damning evidence was the result of the second post-mortem of the body which showed beyond any doubt that death had been caused by strangulation. How this was missed in the original examination caused some conjecture as the shawl was so tight that it had to be cut from the neck. Dodds had told the police that he was not at his house at the time Mary Jane died but evidence was brought that he had been seen there between 2.15 and 2.50 pm. He changed his story saying that he had called back to the house at about 2.30 pm to collect a tool but that Mary Jane had been alive when he left a few minutes later.

Dodds's defence counsel tried to show that Mary's shawl had become twisted around her neck as she had fallen into the fire. The metal stays from Mary's corset were found under the fire grate which meant that she would have had to have actually sat on the fire accidentally which was highly unlikely.

That Dodds had lied to the police and had certainly been instrumental in his wife's death was not in dispute but the jury had to decide whether he had deliberately strangled her with the shawl or whether it had been an accident in which case he would be guilty of manslaughter. The jury brought in a verdict of guilty of wilful murder and sentence of death was passed. Dodds was the first man under sentence of death to appeal under the new Criminal Appeal Act but this was unsuccessful and the death sentence remained in place. He was hanged on Wednesday 5 August by Henry and Thomas Pierrepoint.

In a rather strange coincidence Dodds was not the only one of Mary Jane's husbands to hang. Her first husband had committed suicide – by hanging himself!

CHAPTER 9

Death of an Innocent
1909

Jeremiah O'Conner worked as a miner at the Stanley pit. The fifty-two year old lodged, along with another man, Michael Brown, at the home of Thomas Donnelly and his family at 11 Peel Street, West Stanley. The two lodgers slept in the same room as the Donnellys' two children, a boy and a girl. O'Conner had been living with the family for about three years and ten-year-old Mary had become quite close to him. Besides liking a good drink now and again, the lodgers had never given the family any problems.

On Monday 14 December 1908, O'Conner was not fit to go to work after a weekend drinking binge. That evening at about

The village of West Stanley where Jeremiah O'Conner lodged with the Donnelly family in 1909. Author's collection

8.45 he was seen walking down the lane with Mary. When they failed to return home the police were called. On Friday, Mrs Boyd, who lived at Gibside, contacted the police and told them that on the previous day a man had turned up at her door begging food. The man, who fitted O'Conner's description, had been acting very oddly and seemed extremely shaken. He had told Mrs Boyd that a navvy (labourer) had attacked him and showed her wounds to his arms. He returned to her cottage on the Friday morning and she told him he should go to the police whereupon he had run off. The police moved the search to the area in which the man had been seen and very soon found O'Conner near Tonfield.

Meanwhile the search for the little girl continued. Her badly mutilated body was found on Sunday 20 December under a hedge at Pea Farm, which was a few miles from her home. Mary had been brutally, sexually assaulted and stabbed with a sharp instrument. Her injuries had been so severe she had almost been disembowelled. O'Conner was still in custody and was now charged with murder.

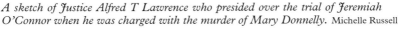

A sketch of Justice Alfred T Lawrence who presided over the trial of Jeremiah O'Connor when he was charged with the murder of Mary Donnelly. Michelle Russell

The trial was held at Durham Assizes on Monday 1 February 1909 before Justice Alfred Tristram Lawrence with CF Lowenthal and H Mundahi for the prosecution and Kevin Marshall for the defence. O'Conner's version of events was that he had been attacked by an Irish navvy and when he tried to protect Mary, the man had cut him with a knife before taking the little girl away. The prosecution pointed out that if this story was true then why did he hide in the fields instead of going straight to the police? Medical opinion was given that the wounds on O'Conner's arms had been self-inflicted. The jury brought in a verdict of guilty and sentence of death was passed.

O'Conner had served in the Royal Irish Fusiliers and the Durham Militia and had two daughters and a son living in Haswell. His children visited him a few days before his execution. He never admitted his guilt but did not take advantage of the new Criminal Court of Appeal and went to his death with quiet resignation. He was hanged on Tuesday 23 February 1909 by Henry Pierrepoint and William Willis.

While O'Conner was incarcerated in Durham Gaol awaiting his execution a search for bodies was still taking place after a disastrous explosion at the West Stanley pit on 16 February. Many of the families living in the area were in deep mourning as the final count of the death toll came to 168 men and boys. Amongst the dead were eighteen-year-old Francis Donnelly of 7 Peel Street and thirty-four-year-old John Donnelly of Beamish Street. It is probable that these were members of the same family who had already suffered the terrible loss of a little girl.

The Lodger, 1909

Abel Atherton, a miner, had lodged with the Patrick family at 20 Thames Street, Chopwell for about two years. Jacob and Elizabeth Ann Patrick had two sons and two daughters. As one of the daughters, Frances, turned fifteen, problems arose within the household because of the over zealous attention twenty-nine-year-old Atherton was paying to her. Eventually Elizabeth Patrick told him to seek other accommodation. Atherton moved to Isabella Forster's house in Mercy Street but he continued to

pay frequent visits to the Patrick household. He was furious at
being forced to move and slandered the family to anyone who
would listen telling them that Jacob was sexually abusing his
daughter.

On the morning of Wednesday 11 August, before leaving
the house, Atherton showed his landlady, Isabella, three gun
cartridges and told her that one was for Jacob Patrick, one for
Francis and the last for himself. That same evening he visited
the Patricks' house telling Elizabeth that her husband was sleeping with her daughter. Elizabeth knew these were malicious lies
and would hear none of it. She told Atherton to leave and come
back when Jacob was there to accuse him to his face. Atherton
then returned to Mercy Street and collected his gun. Isabella
tried to stop him leaving the house with the weapon but he
threatened to shoot her. He made his way back to Thames
Street where Elizabeth, Frances, one of the sons and a neighbour, Mrs Marley, were sitting in the kitchen. When Elizabeth
saw the gun she jumped up, presumably to try to take it from
him, but in the struggle that followed the gun went off. As the
first shot went into the air Frances and Mrs Marley took hold of
Atherton but the gun went off a second time hitting Elizabeth
in the side. When Atherton realised that she was fatally
wounded he took a knife from his pocket and drew it across his
own throat. He then staggered from the house and, on meeting
a police constable at the top of Blyth Street, told him that
Elizabeth was dead. Atherton was arrested and his wound,
which was only superficial, was attended to.

The trial took place at Durham Assizes on Wednesday
10 November before Justice John Lawson Walton with CF
Lowenthal and AJ Lawrie acting for the prosecution and Morgan
Griffiths-Jones for the defence. Atherton stated that he had
only taken his gun from his lodgings to sell it as he was short
of money. He had decided to call into the Patrick household
on his way to the pawn shop and Elizabeth had seen the gun
and panicked. He maintained that, although he had been the
instigator of the events that took place, Elizabeth had been shot
by accident when they were grappling for possession of the gun.
None of the parties present in the kitchen had actually seen who
had pulled the trigger but they had all seen Elizabeth grab the

barrel of the gun. A firearms' expert thought that it was highly unlikely Elizabeth had shot herself giving the distance the gun had been fired from. This was deduced by the powder marks on her clothes and the nature of the wound. Francis Patrick testified that Atherton had made numerous advances towards her which she had rejected. When she had told her parents how serious Atherton's approaches were becoming they had asked him to leave the house. The jury did not believe that Atherton was not intent on revenge and they found him guilty of wilful murder.

Henry Pierrepoint arrived in Durham on the afternoon before the execution was to take place. He called in at the hotel opposite the prison and was talking to the landlord when Atherton's father and sister-in-law came in. They had been visiting him and had some letters that he had written. Their conversation revolved around their belief that Atherton was innocent. Pierrepoint took a seat until they left and, allowing a few minutes, also left and made for the prison. Atherton's relatives were standing outside. They had perhaps guessed that he was to be the executioner and were watching to see if he entered the prison.

The village of Chopwell where Abel Atherton murdered Elizabeth Patrick in 1909.
Author's collection

The morning of Wednesday 8 December dawned clear and frosty. The usual procedure by Pierrepoint and his assistant, William Willis, was followed and as Atherton was led from his cell he seemed fairly composed. At the last moment, as Henry Pierrepoint adjusted the noose around the condemned man's neck, Atherton said, in a husky voice: 'Yer hanging an innocent man.' The white cap was hurriedly drawn over his head and within seconds Atherton was dead. Pierrepoint must have been affected by Atherton's final words as he later recorded the event in his diary concluding with his thought at the time: 'Whether or not, I could not flinch from my duty.' Three representatives of the press had been present and one had heard Atherton speak and included the statement in the report of the execution.

CHAPTER 10

He Waited Seven Years
1910

Thomas Crake, alias Craig, was a former miner, originally from Spennymoor. In the spring of 1903 he began courting Annie Finn who lived at Barnard Castle. In summer of that same year Crake was sentenced to seven years' imprisonment for a misdemeanor. He asked his girlfriend to wait for him and she promised that she would. She kept up the courtship and wrote to Crake in Portland Gaol until September of 1909. Annie then stopped writing as she had met and begun courting twenty-five-year-old Thomas William Henderson who she married on 5 February 1910. She had asked her sister, Winifred, to write and tell Crake of her impending marriage. Even though Crake had received a letter from Winifred with the news, just before he was given parole, he wrote to Annie saying that he hoped they could continue the relationship where they had left off. The letter contained veiled threats against her if he found she had not stayed true to him. Annie

The town of Gateshead where Thomas Crake murdered Annie Finn in 1910.
Author's collection

did not reply to the letter but told her family she was frightened by Crake's jealousy.

Upon his release, on Thursday 24 March 1910, Crake made his way towards Barnard Castle to look for Annie. Winifred would not divulge her sister's whereabouts but he was eventually able to establish that she worked at East Street in Gateshead. Following the trail, he found his way to Thomas' mother's house, 11 Oakwellgate, Gateshead. Mary Jane Henderson assumed Crake was a friend of her son's and pointed out the house where he lived which was further up the same road, number 60. When Crake knocked on the door he was invited in and Henderson arose from his chair to shake the visitor's hand. Crake pulled a revolver from his clothing and shot them both. Annie was shot twice and suffered severe injuries from which she later recovered but Thomas Henderson died shortly after being shot. The perpetrator made his escape and although the police launched an immediate manhunt it was to be almost a month later before he was apprehended.

On 16 April, a report came in of a house and a farmhouse having been broken into and a man having been seen who appeared to be sleeping rough. The police descended on the

An extract from a map showing the location of Oakwellgate where Thomas Crake shot and killed Thomas Henderson in 1910. Ordnance Survey: Newcastle and Gateshead 1894

area and found Crake in a hayloft at Dilston Cottage Farm. He had severe scars to his face so was easily recognisable. Crake stated that he had carried out the act because of provocation but had not meant to kill Henderson, only injure him.

His trial was held at Durham Assizes, on Saturday 25 June, before Justice William Grantham with Bruce Williamson and James Willoughby Jardine acting for the prosecution and Morgan Griffith-Jones for the defence. Crake was found guilty but with a recommendation to mercy because of the circumstances. Although the recommendation was sent to the Home Secretary there was to be no reprieve and twenty-four-year-old Crake walked to the scaffold with a firm step. He was executed on Tuesday 12 July 1910 by Henry Pierrepoint and William Willis. Afterwards Crake's father asked for the revolver because it was the only thing his son had left in his will. The request was refused because the document was made after Crake had been sentenced so the revolver was the property of the Crown.

CHAPTER 11

An Unwanted Rival
1914

Robert Upton, who was fifty and worked as a painter's labourer, lived at Back Albion Street, Jarrow with his fourteen-year-old son, Joseph. He had been acquainted with sixty-four-year-old Charles Gribbin for some time and the two men had a bit of a reputation for being heavy drinkers. In 1911 Upton had met Elizabeth Burden, a woman who had been separated from her husband for twenty years. He introduced Elizabeth to Gribbin and about six months after the introduction she began visiting him also. Gribbin lived at 42 Stanley Street and Elizabeth spent her week divided between each of the men, 'housekeeping'. In 1913 Upton and his son moved in with Gribbin so Elizabeth must have decided that this

The town of Jarrow where Robert Upton and his son lived in 1914. Author's collection

situation was not going to work well for her. She announced
that she was seeing another man, Jack Bloy, and was going to
live with him. Upton threatened her saying that she would
neither have Gribbin or any other man and that he would 'do
for the pair of them'.

On the night of Saturday 20 December, Gribbin returned to
Stanley Street and fell asleep on the floor in a drunken stupor.
Upton followed soon after, also much the worse for wear. In
the early hours of the following morning Upton's son Joseph
was disturbed by the sound of fighting. When he arose he saw
his father on top of Gribbin with a razor in his hand. Joseph
managed to pull his father off but Upton shook free and
attacked Gribbin again. He dragged the razor over Gribbin's
throat three times, inflicting serious wounds. Joseph ran screaming into the neighbour's room. James Evans went to investigate
and saw Gribbin lying on the floor with blood pumping from
his throat. There was no sign of Upton so Evans tied a cloth
around the bleeding man's neck and then ran to the police
station for help. Meanwhile Mrs Evans and Joseph were sitting
horror stricken when Upton suddenly appeared in the room
asking for James Evans. He then began hacking at his own
throat with the razor saying: 'I have done it now. I have done it
to old Charlie now'. Mrs Evans and Joseph tried to rush out but
Upton barred their way. They turned and ran for another door
which took them out into the street.

Police and a doctor were soon at the scene but it was too late
for Gribbin. His main artery had been severed and he had bled
to death within a matter of minutes. Upton was seriously injured
and was taken to the Workhouse hospital where his wounds
were attended to.

Upton admitted to the murder, saying he was so drunk he
did not know what he was doing. Once his condition improved
he stood trial at Durham Assizes on Thursday 5 March 1914,
before Justice Ridley with Bruce Williamson and Mr Armitage
for the prosecution and Hugh O'Neill for the defence. Elizabeth
Burden, now married to Jack Bloy, and Joseph Upton gave evidence. Upton was found guilty of wilful murder and sentenced
to death.

No effort was made for a reprieve and Upton was hanged at a private execution on Tuesday 24 March 1914 by John Ellis and William Willis. A rope had arrived with a condition from the Home Office. It had been thoroughly tested and was to be returned in the same condition as received. Because Upton still had a raw wound to his throat Ellis decided to place the noose in a different position to avoid any mishaps or unnecessary suffering to the condemned man. The knot was usually placed under the left ear which would throw the chin backwards during the fall. On this occasion the knot was placed behind the ear so that the head would be thrown forward onto the chest preventing the wound from opening. The method was a success in that Upton's death was instantaneous.

Previously the body of the hanged man had been left for an hour and then cut down. Now, with new rules that had come into force, instead of leaving the body to hang for an hour, it was to be drawn up to the floor of the execution chamber and the rope removed from the neck. Upton's body was buried within the enclosure of Durham Gaol. This was the year that Durham Gaol took heed of the policies of other gaols and excluded the Press from witnessing any further executions.

This tragedy was certainly touched with a cruel twist of fate. Two men had died for the love of a woman who did not care for either of them and had married another before her admirers were cold in their graves.

A view of a quiet street in Jarrow. Author's collection

CHAPTER 12

Nelson Street, Gateshead 1915

Twenty-one-year-old Nana Barrett, whose real name was Lena Spoors, had moved from her mother and father's house in Lower Cuthbert Street, Gateshead in about 1911. She had had a relationship with a man named Joseph Bell and it was known that she gave birth to a baby that had died.

In about February 1915, Nana started a relationship with thirty-one-year-old Frank Steele, a powerfully built man about six feet in height. They moved into a single room at 31 Nelson Street, Gateshead and lived as man and wife. On the early afternoon of Sunday 16 May the couple were seen together by neighbours. On Sunday, at about 5 pm, Steele met one of his

The town of Gateshead where Nana Barrett was murdered by Frank Steele in 1915.
Author's collection

mates, William Johnson, at Armstrong's works in Gateshead. Steele was drunk and told Johnson that he 'had done Nana in'. Over the next couple of days he repeated this confession to various acquaintances two or three times but for some inexplicable reason nobody paid any attention.

Steele slept at Nelson Street on Sunday and Monday nights and was seen to lock the door as he left in the mornings. The neighbours were suspicious when they realised they had not seen Nana since Sunday and the blinds were drawn at her room window. They tried the door but it was locked and still no one thought to inform the police. On Tuesday, Steele visited his mother and told her he had killed Nana. At last someone took him seriously and the police were called. When they broke into the room at Nelson Street Nana's body was found lying on the bed. A doctor was called and he stated there was no sign of there having been a struggle. Nana had died from loss of blood from a cut throat and she had been dead for at least twenty-four hours. This coincided with Steele's confession to Johnson so it would seem the murder had been committed before 5 pm on Sunday.

Steele stood trial for murder at Durham Assizes on Tuesday 6 July before Justice Ridley with CF Lowenthal and J Scott-Fox for the prosecution and SO Rowan Hamilton for the defence. The prosecution stated that the reason for the murder was jealousy which had been aggravated by the consumption of alcohol. It was found that Nana's ex-boyfriend, Bell, had visited her at Nelson Street and she had then written a letter to him. Steele had read the contents which apparently caused him to become very upset.

Elizabeth Gray, who lived at 33 Nelson Street, was called as a witness and testified that she had heard the voices of the couple

A sketch of Justice Ridley who passed down the death sentence on Frank Steele in 1915. Michelle Russell

in their room on the Sunday afternoon. She had then seen Steele leave by himself but had never set eyes on Nana again. Other witnesses that Steele had spoken to about 'doing Nana in' were called. His defence said that because he was sodden with drink he should only be charged with manslaughter as he was not in control of his actions. No witnesses came forward to speak on Steele's behalf. The jury decided that Steele was wholly responsible for Nana's death and found him guilty of wilful murder and sentence of death was passed. Steele complained that he had not had a fair trial but Justice Ridley stated that, in his opinion, the trial had been thoroughly fair and he should spend the time left to him making his peace with God who might pardon him for the crime because none in the courtroom could. He was hanged on Wednesday 11 August 1915 by John Ellis.

CHAPTER 13

The Monkwearmouth Murder 1916

Joseph Deans had been in South Africa for seventeen years as a soldier and, after his discharge, had worked as a gold miner. He had two pensions, one from the South African Government and one from the South African War Department, for his services in the Imperial Light Horse, amounting to £2 10s (£2.50) a week. When Deans was forty-four he returned to Britain where he met and began courting Catherine Convery. She was forty-eight and a widow who lived with her two daughters and her mother in Devonshire Street near to the *Grey Horse* public house in Monkwearmouth. During the courtship Deans lavished all his money on his sweetheart but, at some point, he found out that she was seeing someone else.

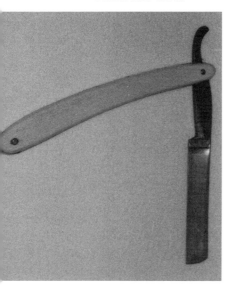

On Friday 6 October 1916, Catherine staggered into the *Grey Horse* with blood pouring down her face and clothes. She was heard to shout: 'He has murdered me this time!' Somehow the injured woman managed, with several of the customers assisting her, to walk to the hospital. She had terrible injuries to the top of her head, a severe wound to the back of her neck and one on her right shoulder. One of the cuts had displaced bone. These injuries had been inflicted with an axe. Catherine died on 13 October.

A razor such as the one Joseph Deans used to try to and cut his own throat after attacking Catherine Convery with an axe in 1922. The author

The doctors who examined Catherine thought that the only way that she had managed to walk to the hospital with such horrific wounds was due to the influence of drink. Deans, meanwhile, had tried unsuccessfully to cut his own throat with a razor. He was taken into custody and when Catherine died was charged with her murder. On the way to the police station he had said that Catherine had had hundreds of pounds from him and had then wanted to 'toss him over'.

At his trial at Durham Assizes, on Wednesday 15 November, before Justice Low with HS Cautley for the prosecution and W Cambier for the defence, the story of a jealous and violent relationship unfurled. The prosecution described how Catherine had taken a soldier home and when Deans found out he had struck her with a coal rake. Her injuries were so severe that they were treated at the infirmary for nine months after the incident. Another time Catherine's daughter had seen Deans strike her mother and then pick up a knife and threaten that 'he would do it now'.

At the beginning of October, Catherine was seen running with Deans chasing her with a piece of thick string in his hand. Catherine was shouting that he was going to choke her. On 5 October, Deans had taken out a gun license from the Dundee post office. He then went to Messrs Wanless' establishment in Sunderland and asked to buy a revolver. He had asked the assistant, Mr Garrick, if the revolver he was shown would kill a man. He was told that it would not and was shown a longer revolver. Deans asked again if it would kill a man. Mr Garrick became worried thinking that his customer may be drunk so asked him to return later. Deans returned the following day, so Mr Garrick put him off by giving him an exemption certificate to be signed by the chief constable. On the same day, a man named Thompson was standing on the corner near the *Wheat Sheaf* when Deans had approached him and offered to sell him a watch, chain and two rings saying they were no good to him. Then, to Thompson's surprise, Deans had removed his hat and showed him a photograph that was inside. The image was of Catherine and Deans had said he loved every inch of her but he was going to finish her off that night.

The following day, Thompson had gone to Catherine and told her what Deans had said. On 6 October, in the *Grey Horse*, Deans had called Thompson over and given him a ring. When Thompson asked what it was for Dean told him it was a keepsake because he could not stand things any longer and he was going to do away with her tonight. After leaving Thompson Deans had gone into an ironmonger's shop and purchased a chopping axe for 2s 6d (13p). That evening Catherine was on her way to the butcher's shop when Deans had called out to her: 'You won't be alive tonight. I won't do it while the daughters are there. I will do it when nobody's there.' Deans then went to a house and paid a debt he owed. Whilst in the house he produced a brown paper parcel containing a chopping axe. He then produced a razor saying: 'The axe is for the lady, the razor for myself.' Deans then returned to the *Grey Horse* where he had a glass of beer and then left. It was shortly after this that Catherine appeared with blood pouring profusely from her wounds.

The defence argued that Deans truly loved the woman and had killed her in a moment of insanity, so the verdict should be manslaughter. This was disproved by all the evidence of previous violence and threats that had been made against Catherine. The judge and jury decided that Dean's actions had been premeditated so it was murder.

Deans was found guilty and, when asked if he had any statement to make, he drew himself up to his full height and declared: 'I killed the woman and I am pleased I killed her.' Justice Low then pronounced a sentence of death.

Dean's defence counsel travelled to London to be heard at the Appeal Court but it was decided there were no grounds for a reprieve because Dean had shown intent and no remorse by saying he was pleased he had killed the woman.

The morning of Wednesday 20 December 1916 dawned cold and cheerless when Deans was woken to be attended by the Rev D Jacob. After eating a hearty breakfast his arms were pinioned by John Ellis, assisted by George Brown. Ellis later recorded in his memoirs that as he led the procession towards the scaffold at the customary pace he heard a clattering of noisy footsteps behind him. On turning he was shocked to see it was Deans pulling his escorts along beside him at almost a run. The elderly chaplain had to place his hand on his shoulder to encourage him to slow down. Deans' haste to reach the scaffold suggested he was a man disillusioned with life and more than ready to die. As the cap was pulled over his head Ellis said that Deans' eyes were 'shining with what seemed to be excitement' and there was a look of 'contented anticipation' on his face. His remains were interred within the prison walls.

CHAPTER 14

To Stop Her Leaving
1920

At Durham Assizes on Thursday 4 March 1920, William Hall stood trial for the murder of Mary Ann Dixon at Sunderland on 6 November 1919. The case was heard before Justice Bailhache with SO Hamilton and Mr Mortimer for the prosecution and C Paley Scott for the defence. Hall was sixty-six and had worked as a brass-finisher until recent years when he had worked as a day labourer in a Sunderland ship-building yard and lived at 34 Moorgate Street in Sunderland. At first his plea was guilty with provocation but then he changed his plea to not guilty.

The facts that emerged were that he had lived off and on for about two years with Mary Ann Dixon. She was a widow of

The town of Sunderland where William Hall murdered Mary Ann Dixon in 1920.
Author's collection

about fifty-five who did not seem to take the relationship as seriously as Hall. Mary Ann kept leaving him and the quarrels that arose between them were due to her treatment of Hall rather than his treatment of her. When Mary Ann left, according to Hall, she would take with her food and other sundries from their home. She had also pawned clothes and the wedding ring Hall had bought for her.

In September 1919, Mary Ann left once again, this time taking a job as a 'night woman' at a lodging house in Grey Street, which greatly upset Hall. On Friday 5 November, Hall went to see his sister, Elizabeth Adamson, and told her that he had just seen Mary Ann and that he was meeting her later on that day. A neighbour, Mrs Hedley, was in the room at the time and saw Hall draw his hand across his throat. Mr Hedley also said he had a wild look and appeared very downhearted, even strange.

Later that evening, Mary Ann and Hall were seen drinking together in the *Tynemouth Castle* public house. Those that saw them thought that they seemed to be on friendly terms. Elizabeth was worried about her brother's state of mind so she went to his house that night at about 10 pm and listened at the door. She heard the couple talking amicably so left and returned to her own home. The following morning, Elizabeth returned twice to find the shutters drawn and the door fastened with a piece of string. She became anxious and went for the police who, on entering found Mary Ann's body upon the bed. There was a large knife wound to her neck and two knives were found in the room. There was an indentation on the bed as if someone else had lain there recently. On the table was a red American cloth with 'All for Jack' chalked upon it. Jack was Hall's brother. There were also a couple of insurance books on the table so it was assumed the writing was in the form of a will.

Hall was eventually found hiding in the water closet at his brother's house. When he was arrested he admitted to killing Mary Ann and trying to cut his own throat. He told the police that they had lain together all night but in the morning she had told him she was leaving him and was going back to the lodging house so he had killed her.

Elizabeth gave evidence as to what had occurred and added that of the two Mary Ann was the worst for drinking. Hall's defence tried to get the charge reduced to manslaughter with extreme provocation but he was found guilty of wilful murder. When asked if he had anything to say he replied: 'If there is anything gained in what I have done, I could stand under God and say there is nothing lost because she was a dead wrong woman.' When the death sentence was pronounced by Justice Bailhache, Hall received the news with: 'Thank you My Lord.'

William Hall was hanged by John Ellis, assisted by Robert Baxter, on Tuesday 23 March 1920.

He Used a Poker, 1920

James and Mary Riley had been married for twenty years and lived at West Auckland. Riley was fifty and worked as a miner. He had served with the forces in India and since his return the relationship was fraught with quarrels. The police were often called because of Riley's violence towards his wife. He had even uttered death threats towards her in front of the police.

On the afternoon of Friday 8 October, Mary had gone to visit her sister and that was the last time she was seen alive. On the following morning Riley had gone to the house of Mr and Mrs Wade and told them that he had killed his wife. Mr Wade went to the Riley's house and found that Mary was indeed dead. He went back to his own house and told Riley that he would have to inform the police. Riley, who at the time was wearing a bloodstained shirt, asked Wade to wait until he got away.

When the police were called they found Mary lying on the floor fully clothed except for her skirt and shoes. In the fireplace were what looked like the remains of her shoes and a piece of burnt material that resembled the material of the coat she had been wearing the previous day. The reason for these items being burnt was never discovered. There were a considerable amount of bloodstained footsteps on the stairs and a picture on the wall that was over six feet (2 m) above the floor was also covered in spots of blood.

Riley was found at Coundon Grange and arrested. By this time he had changed his shirt but when he removed his boots it was found that the stockings on his feet were caked in blood.

The village of West Auckland where James and Mary Riley lived in 1920.
Author's collection

When questioned about the blood on his feet Riley said he had been 'splodging'. He then said that he had quarrelled with his wife during the night and had pushed her. Mary had fallen against the press and when he was woken the following morning by the milk boy Riley had found her dead. The police found no evidence of blood upon the press. Riley had been drinking in a public house the previous evening and it was believed he had returned home drunk and attacked his wife. No one except Riley knew what had really taken place but the evidence pointed to Riley beating Mary with a poker. This would explain the splattering of blood on the picture.

His trial was heard at Durham Assizes on Saturday 13 November before Justice Rigby Swift with WJ Waugh and S Fleming acting for the prosecution and Mr Mortimer and CP Scott for the defence. After all the evidence was heard the jury returned a verdict of guilty of wilful murder. John Hall, the jury foreman, put forward a recommendation for mercy but the Home Secretary found no grounds for a reprieve. Riley was hanged by Thomas Pierrepoint, assisted by Edward Taylor, on Tuesday 30 November 1920. When the inquest took place on the body the coroner remarked that Riley was not the usual class that the court had to deal with. He had voluntarily joined the forces and served his country but, sadly, instead of being entitled to a soldier's funeral he would be buried as a felon within the walls of the prison.

CHAPTER 15

The Late Post
1922

James Hutton Williamson, a thirty-seven-year-old miner, his wife, Mary, and their five children lived at Easington Colliery. Williamson had been ill-treating his wife for many years so, in December 1921, she left him. Mary and her five children moved in with her parents at Houghton-le-Spring. On 17 December, she obtained a separation order and Williamson was ordered to pay her 30s (£1.50p) a week for the support of his wife and children. The money was to be paid to the magistrates' clerk who would then forward it by post to Mary. Williamson was angry about his wife leaving and even angrier at the police court proceedings. He had said to

Easington Colliery where James Williamson, his wife, Mary and their five children had lived up until the couple separated in 1922. Author's collection

one of his daughters: 'The next time I put my hands on your mother you will never see her face again. I'll do away with her.' A neighbour of his wife's parents had also heard him say that he 'would do his wife in'.

On Thursday 29 December 1921, Williamson visited his wife and stayed over the New Year. Although they were getting along well Mary refused to return home with her husband. On Friday 6 January 1922, Williamson again visited Mary staying the night and sleeping on a mat in front of the kitchen fire where Mary and the children also slept on a shake down. The following morning Mary waited for the post and when her support money did not arrive as it should have, she started arguing with her husband accusing him of not paying. Williamson told her that he had paid but Mary did not believe him. A little later Mary's parents left the house. They had not been gone long when, witnessed by two of their children, Williamson jumped up, put his hand over Mary's face, pulled her head back and cut her throat with a razor. The children fled from the house and alerted neighbours. As one of the neighbours entered he saw Williamson kneeling at Mary's side sawing at her throat with the razor. Two more men entered the house and Williamson said to them: 'I have done it this time. It's what I have been waiting for for a long time.'

Dr Boyd was called and when he arrived to examine Mary, Williamson told him not to bother as she was dead. The doctor later testified that it was obvious that there had been repeated attempts to sever the already dead woman's neck. Williamson was arrested for his wife's murder and committed for trial at Durham Assizes on Wednesday 1 March before Justice Bray with EA Mitchell-Innes for the prosecution and CP Scott for the defence.

A sketch of Justice Bray, who passed down sentence of death on James Williamson for the murder of his wife.
Michelle Russell

There had been no need for that final argument between the couple. Williamson had paid the support money. Due to a delay caused by the Christmas and New Year holidays the money arrived two days after the crime had been committed. At the trial it transpired that Williamson's father had committed suicide by hanging himself, one of his sisters had died in an insane asylum and another had been, for a time, an inmate of a mental institution. Williamson's defence tried to plead insanity but this was overturned when Dr Robert Stuart, who was the medical officer for Durham Gaol, stated that he had monitored Williamson since his arrest. In his opinion there was no evidence of insanity. The jury then found Williamson guilty of wilful murder. On the death sentence being pronounced Williamson saluted Justice Bray and thanked him.

There was a light fall of snow on Tuesday 21 March 1922 when Thomas Pierrepoint, assisted by William Willis, hanged James Williamson.

CHAPTER 16

Five Shots
1923

Daniel Cassidy was a blacksmith by trade and he and his wife, Elizabeth, had lived in Manchester but moved to Sunderland. In about 1917, Elizabeth had left her husband and moved back to Manchester. The couple had two married daughters, Elizabeth Quinn and Agnes Hodgson. Cassidy lived with twenty-year-old Elizabeth and her husband, Bernard, who was thirty. Opposite, in the upper rooms at 1 Woodbine Street in Hendon, lived Agnes and her husband. Towards the end of 1922 Mrs Cassidy had written to her daughter to say she was returning to Sunderland on 14 December and would stay with the Hodgsons over the Christmas period. Cassidy met his wife on several occasions throughout her visit and the two seemed to be on amicable terms. On Sunday 31 December, Cassidy had gone to the Hodgson's house and asked his daughter if he could borrow 6d (3p). Agnes said she did not have any money but could borrow it for him. Cassidy answered that it did not matter 'but tell that b. . . . . . she is looking for trouble. I have been down Millfield and heard a tale'. After making these comments referring to his wife he left the house.

The following night, which was the first night of 1923, there was a family party at the house in Woodbine Street. Quinn was sitting in a basket chair playing his accordion in the company of his wife, mother-in-law, Agnes and two children. There was a knock on the door and Agnes shouted the caller to come in. When there was no response Elizabeth Cassidy went to open the door. As she did so her husband burst in firing a revolver. Five shots were fired altogether. Quinn slumped back in his chair with blood pouring from his nose and mouth. He must have died instantly from two bullets to his body. Cassidy's wife was shot in the chest and their daughter, Elizabeth, took a bullet to her abdomen. James Coggin, who lived in another part of the house, heard the gunfire and rushed in. He attacked Cassidy who retaliated by hitting him across the head with the butt of the revolver. Coggin managed to wrestle the weapon from Cassidy's grasp and return the blow overpowering his opponent. The two injured women were taken to Newcastle infirmary in a critical condition where they both later recovered. Cassidy stood trial at Durham Assizes on Friday 23 February before Justice Roche for the murder of Quinn and the attempted murder of his wife and daughter. Walter Hedley and RF Burnand acted for the prosecution and J Charlesworth for the defence.

Cassidy said that he had found out his wife had been living with a Jew in Manchester. When she returned to Sunderland she had poisoned the minds of his family against him and he had only gone to the house to upset the party and had not intended to shoot anyone. When he realized that he had caused injury he was going to shoot himself but was overpowered before he could do so. Agnes said that while living in Manchester her father had been detained for a time in an asylum but had eventually been released as sane. Superintendent Ruddick, who had carried out an investigation, stated that it was true that Cassidy had been detained in a mental ward. Although he did not drink he was thought of as a man of peculiar habits. Cassidy told the court that his wife had lied to get him put away. Dr Robert Stuart had visited Cassidy while he was in Durham Gaol. In his opinion the sixty-year-old man was in bad physical health but was perfectly rational and sane. The jury returned a verdict of guilty of wilful murder and attempted murder and Justice Roche sentenced him to death. Cassidy's defence took the case to the Criminal Appeal Court in London but a reprieve was denied.

It was reported that although Cassidy had spent a restless night he was resigned to his fate as he took his last walk on Tuesday 3 April 1923, hanged by Thomas Pierrepoint.

The Wedding's Off, 1923

Jane Nagi, nee Brown, was the English widow of an Arabian seaman and worked at a restaurant at East Holburn, South Shields owned by Salem Ali. She had met and become engaged to another Arab seaman, Hassen Mohamed. The date of the wedding was set for Wednesday 14 March. On the afternoon of Monday 12 March Jane turned up for work but was told to go home as she had been drinking. She said she would wait for her fiancé. About an hour later, Mohamed appeared and the two began to argue with Jane telling him their relationship was over. The argument became violent when she attacked Mohamed, scratching his face and grabbing at his throat. The police were called and, after a warning, Jane seemed to calm down. Mohamed must have thought everything was now okay and asked Jane if their relationship could be on again. She said no so Mohamed left the restaurant. A few minutes later Jane was dead and Mohamed was arrested for her murder.

The trial was held at Durham Assizes on Tuesday 3 July before Lord Chief Justice Gordon Hewart with LR Lipsett acting for the prosecution and AP Peaker for the defence.

The town of South Shields where Jane Nagi was murdered in 1923 by her fiancée Hassen Mohamed. Author's collection

Witnesses that were present during the episode described what had taken place. After their previous argument Jane was sitting in the kitchen when, a few minutes later, Mohamed returned. He stood at the kitchen door smoking and then calmly pulled out a revolver and shot Jane in the chest. Mohamed gave a different story of the events saying that all the witnesses were lying. He stated that he had seen Jane about 3 pm and they were supposed to meet later at her parents' house. He was then told that she was seeing someone else at the restaurant. When Mohamed arrived Jane was sitting on Salem Ali's knee. He and Ali had a fight in which Ali drew a gun and as Mohamed tried to take possession of the weapon it went off by accident with the bullet hitting Jane. The staff and customers that were in the restaurant restrained the two men and then concocted a story whereby Mohamed was blamed for the shooting. The jury did not believe Mohamed's version and he was found guilty of twenty-five-year-old Jane's murder.

Thirty-three-year-old Hassen Mohamed prayed in his native tongue as he was led to the scaffold on Wednesday 8 August 1923, to be hanged by Thomas Pierrepoint.

CHAPTER 17

She Was Pregnant
1924

atthew Frederick Atkinson Nunn was twenty-four, worked as a miner and lived in Tantobie. He had been courting Minetta Mary Kelly for about three months and in August he asked her mother if they could marry. Minetta's mother agreed as long as that was what her daughter wanted. Minetta and Nunn often entered dancing competitions together and this was how they had got together as a couple. Prior to this relationship Minetta had been courting a man named Joseph Hughes for about five months. Nunn had apparently stepped in and wooed Minetta away from Hughes.

By 8 September 1923, Minetta's mother noticed a coolness between her daughter and Nunn so asked him if there was something wrong with Minetta to which he had replied that there was but had not elaborated. On Monday 10 September, Minetta and Hughes were together when they met Nunn. Hughes suspected that Minetta was pregnant and had said to Nunn: 'Well Matt you have managed to separate us at last.' Nunn had replied: 'I will marry her tomorrow if she is willing.' Hughes replied: 'Yes, so would I. Do you think yourself a man?' Nunn had replied: 'That is the only way I could get her.' Hughes had then answered: 'But you have not got her yet.' On the following day, Minetta admitted to her father that she did not want to marry Nunn. The couple went to Nunn's parents' house and all seemed well between them. They left about 9.30 in the evening with Mrs Nunn telling her son not to be late back and he had answered that he would not be long.

At about 2.30 on the morning of Wednesday 12 September Nunn stumbled into the house of some friends. There was a terrible wound on Nunn's throat. He took some papers from his pocket and placed them on the table before falling to the floor. One of his friends rendered first aid and the police were called. When the police asked Nunn what had happened he said he had run away from Minetta. He then told them that if they went to Bush Blades, across the fields from where they were, they would find Minetta's body. Nunn said that she had cut him and then killed herself. The police found Minetta lying near a thorn hedge with the blade of a razor in her lap. The other half of the razor was lying a few feet away.

On medical examination the doctor found Nunn's windpipe partially severed. The wound inflicted with the razor to Minetta's throat had almost severed her head from her body. The examination also showed that Minetta was pregnant.

Nunn received treatment for his wound and was well enough to stand trial at Durham Assizes before Justice Henry Alfred McCardie on Wednesday 14 November 1923. GFL Mortimer and LR Lipsett acted for the prosecution and Mr Wilson for the defence. The papers he had placed on the table were letters and they were read out in the court. There were three letters, the first was to Minetta and read:

If you marry me you will not regret it as long as you live. I will be content if you will just look after me. If you will not marry me I will not be in the country very long. If you marry that one [Hughes] you will have my dying curse on you both from the day you marry until the day you die.

The second two letters were to his mother and read:

Dear Mother
Don't worry when you have read this letter as I will be all right. Will write you when I get settled down. It may be a few months before you get a letter from me. Edith will tell you the reason I am going away like this. I am getting the hardest knock I will ever get in this life. So don't go down to Tantobie and say anything to Min. Let things stay as they are because she will have a child before long and I will be the father of it. She will never get a pennypiece out from me until she marries me to give the child a name.

Dear Mother
This is the end. Think kindly of me and tell Mrs Kelly I am sorry for it is the only way out of it. I cannot stand it any longer.

It was quite obvious that Nunn had written two of the letters with the intention of leaving the country. The last letter showed that perhaps he intended suicide. Mrs Kelly was called to the stand and told the court that she had said to her husband that their daughter wanted Hughes and not Nunn. She wanted her daughter to marry Nunn as he was regarded as a good, steady fellow. Mrs Kelly said that Minetta had threatened to run away but had never contemplated suicide. Hughes stated that he was not responsible for Minetta's pregnancy but would have married her anyway as long as he had obtained her parent's consent. Dr James Gemmell described the wounds on Nunn and Minetta. In his opinion it was impossible for a girl of Minetta's stature to have inflicted either of the wounds. His statement was backed up by Dr Edward Cecil Brewis, who had been a house surgeon at Newcastle Infirmary. Dr Brewis added that the nature of the wound on Nunn's throat showed that it had been self inflicted.

The jury found a verdict of guilty of wilful murder with a recommendation of mercy and a sentence of death was passed. An appeal was made but was unsuccessful and Matthew Nunn, with the wound to his throat still unhealed, was hanged by Thomas Pierrepoint on Wednesday 2 January 1924.

CHAPTER 18

The Ex-Soldier
1925

argaret Ann Graham left her husband, Henry, in August 1924 and, taking their two-year-old adopted child, she went to live with her mother, Mary Alice Burnett, in Rutland Street, Sunderland. Henry, who was an ex-soldier, had employment as a window cleaner. His wife obtained a separation order and he was ordered to pay her maintenance of 15s (75p) a week. On the afternoon of Sunday 21 December Margaret, her brother-in-law, Robert Dolman and her cousin, John Swan, had been to the hospital to see Margaret's sister. As they were returning home along St Mark's Road, Graham caught up with them. He pulled his wife to one side and they talked quietly for a short time. Margaret was about to rejoin her companions when Graham suddenly punched her on the face. She fell onto one knee and as she did so her husband pulled a dagger from his pocket and stabbed her repeatedly in the back. Dolman tried to interfere but Graham struck at him with the weapon and then ran off down the road chased by a group of men who had witnessed the attack. John Robson lived in Drake Street and, hearing the commotion, ran outside and joined in the chase. He caught up with Graham and managed to persuade him to relinquish the knife. Graham's words to him were:

> *Here it is, I'll tell you all about it. It is my own wife and we have been separated about four months. I have wrote letters trying to make it up to her but she would not come back. I have told her the consequences and it is done now.*

Detective Thomas McManus arrived to take Graham into custody and walked him back to where Margaret was lying at the roadside. The crowd was baying for Graham's blood so McManus thought it prudent to get him away in the ambulance that had arrived to take Margaret to hospital. She did not survive her injuries and Graham was charged with murder.

The trial was held at Durham Assizes on Friday 6 March 1925 before Justice Edward Acton with HS Cautley and Major Ronald Ross acting for the prosecution and GH Wilson-Fox for the defence. Perhaps Graham thought that if it was shown the attack had not been premeditated and he had stabbed his wife in a fit of passion the verdict would be the lesser charge of manslaughter. It may have been to that end that he told the court that he had bought the knife for his child. The prosecution had no trouble convincing the jury that no man would buy such a weapon for a two-year-old and Graham had, by his own statements admitted intent. He had told McManus that he was glad his wife was dead because he now knew where she was. Robson testified as to what Graham had said when he took the knife from him.

The defence put forward an insanity plea stemming from Graham having been injured during the Great War but this was rejected by the medical testimony.

When the jury found him guilty Graham showed no remorse and thanked them for their verdict. He said that he had got his wish and it was a life for a life. Justice Acton then pronounced sentence of death. Despite this bravado at the trial, Graham appealed against his sentence but the appeal was denied.

The Jealous Fiancée, 1925

Twenty-five-year-old Ruth Surtees Rodgers worked as a confidential clerk at the City and Floorcloth Linoleum Company at Newcastle and lived with her widowed mother and an aunt at 30 Abbey Street, Gateshead. Ruth was known as a straightforward, honest and clean living girl. She had been engaged to Thomas Henry Shelton, who worked as a fitter, for about four years and it seemed to all that knew them that they idolised each other.

On the evening of Thursday 29 January 1925 Ruth was leaving work with a young apprentice when Shelton appeared. The couple began walking and talking together and seemed to be on friendly terms. About an hour later a neighbour, Beatrice Ivy Scarth, was returning home with her shopping when she saw the couple ahead of her in Abbey Street. Suddenly Ruth began to run with Shelton chasing after her. Beatrice saw him catch Ruth and then saw her fall on the pavement with him on top of her immediately afterwards. Ruth was carried into her mother's doorway bleeding from a deep wound to her throat. Shelton had cut his own throat and was helped into the house of John and Annie Carr. Neighbours had called the police and a doctor but when they arrived Ruth was dead. Shelton's wound was only superficial and he was taken into custody.

The trial was held at Durham on Thursday 5 March before Justice Acton with GFL Mortimer and Ronald Powell for the prosecution and Archibald Wilson for the defence. Neighbours and friends of the couple were called as witnesses. Walter Pearson told the court that in December 1924 Ruth had shown Shelton a letter that was signed 'Walt'. Shelton asked who it

was from and she had said it was from one of her old boys. Shelton jumped to the conclusion that it was from Walter Shiel, a manager of the company whom Ruth had worked for as a confidential clerk. The couple quarrelled over this and Ruth stopped wearing her engagement ring. Georgina Rodgers, Ruth's sister, told Shelton that he had nothing to worry about as far as Shiel was concerned because he was a married man with three children. She also told the court that Shelton was often bad tempered and could be a tyrant and added that he had been extremely upset over the death of his young brother. Towards the end of January, Shelton had spoken to friends saying that Ruth and he had been all right until Shiel had come on the job. He had

Ruth Surtees Rodgers murdered by Thomas Shelton in at Gateshead in 1925. Author's collection

also said that if he could not have his girl no one else would. He told Mr Taylor, who was a bus driver, that Ruth belonged to him and he belonged to her and if he could not have her he would do her and himself in, he was not afraid of the consequences. Another woman he had spoken to was Hannah Quigley who worked at the Gateshead Co-operative Society. She said that Shelton did not seem himself, had a vacant look and was the picture of misery. John Clemo Trotter was an ex-policeman who now worked as a private detective and he confirmed that Shelton had hired him to keep a watch on Ruth because he suspected her of going to meet another man but before any sort of surveillance was organised Ruth was dead. Walter Shiel denied the suggestion of there being any sort of an improper relationship between himself and Ruth. Lastly, papers that were found in Shelton's pockets were produced of which one was a diary inscribed: 'Things concerning Ruth Rodgers'. The other was a letter to his mother in which he wrote that he would see her in Heaven and that she must not forget to bury him and Ruth together. These showed that his intention was to kill Ruth and then himself.

The defence tried to plead insanity on the grounds that Shelton had not been in his right mind since the death of his little brother. This was disputed by medical evidence. Whether there had been any foundations for his jealousy or not, the fact remained that Shelton had killed Ruth. The jury found him guilty of wilful murder and he was sentenced to death.

At 7.50 am on Wednesday 25 April 1925 forty-two-year-old Henry Graham and Thomas Shelton, who was twenty-five, met each other for the first and last time. Both men had maintained a cheery disposition throughout their incarceration and neither had shown any remorse for their actions. Graham had been visited on the previous day by some friends whom he had told that he was in the best of spirits and would soon be 'with her'. As the Cathedral clock chimed eight the two men were sent to be with their partners by Thomas Pierrepoint and two new assistants, Henry Pollard and Lionel Mann.

CHAPTER 19

Silver Street, Newcastle 1926

J ames Smith, a twenty-three-year-old ship's fireman, was the first person to be convicted at Newcastle Assizes and the execution to take place at Durham. Sadly, Smith's story is short but not so sweet. He was originally from Berwick-upon-Tweed. Smith and his wife, Catherine, did not have a happy marriage and she had left him on more than one occasion because of his terrible jealousy. In February 1926, when she was twenty-six, Catherine left the marital home again and went to live with her sister, Ellen, and her mother, Catherine Scott, in a tenement at 6 Silver Street in Newcastle. Catherine's mother also owned number 23 Silver Street which was let out as rooms. On Saturday 18 April 1926 Mrs Scott went to check on her property and found a gambling session going on with one of the participants being James Smith. She called the police and this must have angered her son-in-law. The next day, Smith and a few other men hurled abuse and threats outside number 6 and the police were called again. On Monday 26 April, Ellen had been on an errand and when she returned Smith and her sister were standing at the stairhead talking. Ellen was with her mother in the kitchen when they heard an agonising scream. They rushed to the stairs and saw Catherine, blood oozing from her chest, being dragged down the stairs by Smith who had a dagger in one hand. Ellen ran for the police but by the time PC Michael Hedley Smith arrived Catherine was dead. Smith had run out of the house but was very soon caught and taken into custody.

The trial was held at Newcastle Assizes on Friday 2 July before Justice George Wright with G Russell Vick for the prosecution and Archibald Wilson for the defence. An insanity plea was put forward with Smith maintaining that he was drunk

The main street of the town of Berwick-upon-Tweed where James Smith was born.
The author

and that he did not know what he was doing but this was discarded by the jury and they brought in a verdict of guilty of wilful murder. A petition was signed for his reprieve but was unsuccessful. Smith was reported to have been an exemplary prisoner and walked to the scaffold with quiet resignation on Monday 10 August 1926 to be hanged by Thomas Pierrepoint assisted by Thomas Phillips.

CHAPTER 20

Out of the Mouths of Babes 1928

J ohn Thomas Dunn's case is unusual because the evidence that helped condemn him was given by his children. Dunn, a miner, and his forty-four-year-old wife Ada Elizabeth had been married for twenty-five years and lived at 2 Lumsden's Buildings in Sacriston. Of their eight children all lived away from home apart from the three youngest. One of their daughters stayed at a school for the blind. The marriage had not been happy for some time and it was common knowledge that Dunn mistreated his wife. On 13 September 1927 Ada decided enough was enough and she went to stay with her mother in Gateshead. Dunn wrote to

The village of Sacriston where John Dunn murdered his wife in 1928.
Author's collection

her, blaming her for the problems they had encountered. The letter was also very threatening and Ada showed it to Sergeant O'Sullivan who visited Dunn at his home and cautioned him. Dunn then wrote another letter telling Ada that the police had spoken to him and he was sorry that he had written the first letter. He went on to beg her to return to him saying he could not live without her. This second letter must have touched Ada's heart because, on Friday 23 September, she returned to her husband but by the following day she was dead.

In the early hours of Saturday morning a neighbour, Arthur Holmes Trainer, was awoken to Dunn shouting for the police. He told Trainer that his wife had committed suicide. When the police arrived they found Ada's body by the back door with deep marks around her neck. Dunn told them that she had often threatened suicide and he had found her hanging from pegs on the wall so had cut her down and drawn the noose off over her head. The police inspected the rope fashioned into a noose that was lying nearby and suggested that it could not have been pulled over her head. His reply was: 'Well I got it off.' Being suspicious of the whole scenario, Dunn was taken into custody whilst further investigations and a medical examination of the body were carried out. When all the evidence came to light he was charged with his wife's murder.

Dunn was committed to stand trial at Durham Assizes on Thursday 15 November 1927 before Justice Roche with CF Lowenthal and CP Scott for the prosecution and Archibald Wilson for the defence. Pleading not guilty, Dunn gave his version of events. He stated that Ada had returned to him but would not sleep in the same room. He had gone to bed in another room and woken just after midnight. Seeing a light on in the kitchen, he had entered and found his wife hanging by a rope from pegs. Dunn then stated that he had cut her body down and removed the noose from her neck and called to the neighbours for help. In his defence, as to his character, he said he had an impeccable record having been twice in the army fighting to protect his country and family and left both times with an honourable discharge. Dunn added that they had a daughter that was blind and if it was not for his persistence she would never have been helped. He told the court that he was a good husband and father and it was his wife that was full of deceit.

The first neighbour to testify was Annie Reay who said that she had been awakened by a rumbling noise and a little later Dunn shouting to her that his wife was dying. When she entered the kitchen she saw Ada stretched out on the floor and obviously dead. When Annie was questioned by Dunn's defence she told the court that Ada had once said to her: 'There is nothing but the river for myself and my children,' which could have pointed to thoughts of suicide.

Sergeant O'Shea told the court of his questioning of Dunn at the scene. He had asked Dunn about the noose which was on the floor. Dunn told the sergeant that he had drawn it over his wife's head after he had cut her body down. O'Shea did some calculations and then told Dunn that it was impossible for him to have removed the noose over Ada's head as it was too small. Later measurements were done on the rope from the pegs to the floor and it was shown that there was not enough height for Ada to have hanged herself as her feet would have touched the floor. Also, the rope marks on Ada's neck were too low to have been caused by hanging. It was established that she had not died in the way Dunn claimed but had been strangled.

One of Dunn's married daughters, Ada Walsh, stated that her parents had not had a happy marriage. On one occasion her father had tried to strangle her mother and had to be pulled away. Sixteen-year-old Thomas said that his parents lived together happily 'only at odd times'.

On the night of the tragedy the three youngest children, including Richard, who was eleven, were in bed upstairs. Richard described what had happened that night by saying that when he went to bed his parents were in the kitchen quarrelling. He heard a stool fall over and then a choking sound. Richard called out and his father answered telling him to go to sleep, that they were only playing. The boy then heard his mother scream and his father shouted at him again to go to sleep there was nothing wrong. Dunn then came upstairs and asked the children if they were okay, closing the bedroom door as he left. This was also confirmed by another of the children, nine-year-old Albert. The next thing Richard heard was his father shouting to him to come down because his mother was dying. Richard was asked whether his father was good to him. He answered: 'Sometimes.' He was then asked whether his father seemed distressed about what had happened. Richard answered: 'He seemed to be, but sometimes he only makes out.'

Dunn was found guilty of wilful murder and sentenced to death. On hearing this young Richard broke away from the people he was with and ran down the street crying piteously that they were going to hang his father. Dunn's sister, Mrs Warren, lodged an appeal on the grounds that her brother had spent some time in Sedgefield asylum and he was not of sound mind at the time of the murder. Two of Dunn's sons also wrote to the Home Secretary appealing for a reprieve which was unsuccessful.

On Friday 6 January 1928, fifty-two-year-old Dunn was hanged by Thomas Pierrepoint. The only notification to the few bystanders that waited outside the gates that the deed had been done was the sound of a bell ringing within the gaol.

The Bank Robber, 1928

The small branch of Lloyds Bank in Ferryhill was replaced by the Cash Boot Store which eventually became part of the *Black Bull Hotel*. It was situated where the lounge of the hotel is at the present time. In 1928, William Byland Abbey, who was thirty-one and of small stature, worked as a cashier at the bank.

It was a common practice in the early twentieth century for one employee to be in sole charge of a small bank and on Thursday 16 February 1928 Abbey was filling this role. Just after 3 pm, which was the time the branch usually closed, passers by were stopped in their tracks when they heard a commotion and then saw a brass weight crash through the window of the bank onto the street. William Kell rushed into the bank to see what was happening and found the cash dispenser open and empty. Abbey was huddled in a corner and, although he was fatally injured, had managed to throw the missile through the window to attract attention to his plight. PC Grieves was quickly on the scene and, before Abbey died, he was able to say only that the attacker was a tall man and that he had taken everything. Blood was splattered everywhere showing that there

The Black Bull Hotel *in Ferryhill, which was next door to the small branch of Lloyds Bank when William Abbey was murdered in 1928.* Author's collection

had been a fierce struggle and Abbey had not given up easily. A bloodstained cobbler's knife was found at the scene.

On a medical examination, Dr James Jack reported that Abbey had five wounds to his forehead caused by a small mallet or hammer and two wounds to his throat that had been inflicted with the cobbler's knife. One of the cuts had gone straight through the neck. More than £200 had been taken and a hunt for the murdering thief was immediately put into motion.

After questioning the people who had been in the area at the time the attack took place a bus conductress, Gladys Turner, pointed them in the direction of a suspect. A man she often spoke to boarded her bus at Metal Bridge at about 3.50 pm on the day of the murder. She had also seen him earlier that day in Ferryhill but when she mentioned this to him he denied that he had been anywhere within the area. Knowing the police were appealing for information on anyone acting suspiciously at that time she came forward. She did not know the man by name but knew he worked as a male nurse at Durham County Asylum in Sedgefield. It did not take the police long to track down and question twenty-two-year-old Norman Elliott. He had married Elizabeth Callan on 18 January 1928 whose parents kept the

Turk's Head, a public house at Kelloe. The couple had moved into cheap lodgings while Elliott still had a room at the asylum because of his night shifts. His wages were £1.4s (£1.20) a week. He had been seen by witnesses in the area of the bank on the day prior to the murder and it was later suggested that he had been inspecting the lay out with a view to robbing the premises the following day. He was also identified by witnesses as having been in the street just before the murder took place. When Elliott's room was searched well over £100 was found, some of the notes bloodstained and many, identified by the serial numbers, were proved to have come from the bank. Small spots of blood were also found on Elliott's clothes and shoes and it was proven that prior to the murder he had been extremely short of money but afterwards had been spending lavishly buying clothes and pieces of furniture.

Elliott pleaded not guilty to both the robbery and the murder when he stood trial at Durham on Tuesday 26 June before Justice Frank Douglas MacKinnon with GFL Mortimer and GHB Streatfield acting for the prosecution and AR Linsley for the defence.

Elliott's story was that when he was on his annual leave in 1927 he had met a man named George Sinclair in London. The two became friends and they travelled to quite a few race meetings together. Sinclair was very good at picking winners and Elliott enjoyed a bet. The week before the crime took place, Elliott had met Sinclair in Durham. Sinclair had told Elliott that he had business in Ferryhill and would meet him at Coxhoe at lunchtime on 16 February. They met up and travelled from Coxhoe to Thinford crossroads and then walked into Ferryhill. Sinclair said that he had been in the village twice that week trying to settle a money matter and he was hoping to sort everything out that day. He then told Elliott that he had to see someone and then would be going to Lloyds' Bank to cash a cheque. Elliott hung about the village for a short time and then went to the bank. He said he had described Sinclair to Mr Abbey and asked if he had seen him. Abbey replied that he had not and it was only ten minutes until the bank would close. Elliott then said he walked to the *Post Boy Hotel* to find Sinclair. When there was no sign of his friend he walked back to the

The village of Ferryhill where the cashier of the branch of Lloyds Bank was robbed and killed. Author's collection

bank. By this time the door to the bank was closed but swung open when pushed. Elliott then felt himself being pulled into the bank. He was confronted by Sinclair who had blood all over his hands and clothes. Sinclair pushed a wad of notes into Elliott's pocket and then left. Elliott then said he heard moaning and saw Abbey lying huddled behind the counter. He went to try and help him by pulling the knife from the injured man's neck but lost his nerve and left. He walked to the crossroads and then boarded a bus without seeing any sign of Sinclair. Elliott worked that night and the following morning he was going to send the money to the police anonymously but he could not bear to touch it so hid it away. £138.10s (£138.50) of the money found by the police he said was his and the rest given to him by Sinclair. Some was money he had saved, some was won on bets and £47.10s (£47.50) was received from a solicitor, Mr Marquis. Elliott said he had been saving to make a home for himself and his wife. The police had shown Elliott photographs of men who had been through their hands but he could not identify any of them as Sinclair.

The prosecution summed up by saying that Elliott was an actor. If his story were true then why had he left the bank and not called for assistance for Abbey and for help in catching the real culprit? To leave the scene and go to work as usual were not the actions of an innocent man. Elliott had been seen in Ferryhill by a number of witnesses but none had seen him in the company of another man. The defence argued that Elliott said that Abbey knew him so why had he not identified him to the police? There was no evidence, however, that the two men were acquainted. Another point that was put forward was that the bloodstains on Elliott's clothes were only spots and not consistent with him having inflicted the terrible injuries on the victim.

The trial lasted two days but the defence could not bring a strong enough case as, although there were some small inconsistencies, the overall evidence against Elliott was overwhelming. The jury agreed that Sinclair was fictitious and the real perpetrator was the man in the dock, so on 27 June they returned a verdict of guilty of robbery and wilful murder. When Justice MacKinnon passed down sentence of death Elliott fainted and had to be carried away. There was an appeal lodged but no reprieve was granted. Maintaining his innocence to the end Norman Elliott was hanged by Thomas Pierrepoint and Robert Wilson on Friday 10 August 1928.

CHAPTER **21**

Buried Alive!
1929

On the afternoon of Saturday 22 September 1928, Annie Stirr was walking along a country lane at Norton when she noticed a mound of freshly dug earth in a ditch at the side of the footpath. Her curiosity aroused as to why anyone would dig in such a spot, she took a closer look and, to her horror, saw a hand protruding from the soil. On raising the alarm the area was excavated to reveal a shallow grave which contained the bodies of a man and a woman. They were both lying on their backs with the man's head resting on the face of the woman. The bodies were soon identified as sixty-two-year-old Thomas Kirby and his wife, Emily Francis Kirby, who was sixty-four. Living at Briargarth, a bungalow on

A postcard of Thornaby Green with the Kirby's house, Briargarth, on the left between the trees. Remembering Thornaby Group

Thornaby Green, which was about four miles from where they were found, they had only been married about five years, their previous partners having passed away.

Emily ran a tripe stall on Stockton market and was known to be in the habit of carrying a considerable amount of money in her handbag. The couple were very comfortably off and had just taken a mortgage on a second house which was rented out. Thomas, as well as assisting his wife on her stall, also worked for a son who was a hardware merchant.

On 18 September, Thomas had received a month's wages of £16 and £6 10s (£6.50p) in rent. He was known to keep his money in a rather distinctive wallet that he had been given to him as a wedding present. No personal possessions were found either on the bodies or in the vicinity of the grave so it was concluded that the motive for the murders was robbery.

On medical examination it was determined that the couple had been rendered unconscious by violent blows to the head inflicted with an object such as a poker. There were no fractures but there was bruising, and some of the wounds had bled. It also appeared that there had been an attempt at strangulation but, although some of the injuries were severe, they were not the cause of death. The conclusion was that the couple had probably been unconscious when they were buried but were certainly still alive. Their windpipes were full of grit showing that they had suffocated under the soil. It was ascertained that they had been dead between eight and twenty hours. There were signs near to where they were found that they had been dragged to their grave through a hedge at the side of the nearby

High Street in Stockton where the Kirby's had a market stall. Author's collection

field. About fifteen feet (approx 5 metres) away from the bodies a spade was found pushed into a hedge.

Police enquiries led them to suspect twenty-two-year-old Charles William Conlin, Emily Kirby's grandson. He lived with his mother, his sister Doris and her husband at 70 Centenary Terrace, Norton Avenue, Stockton and worked part-time at the Synthetic Works in Billingham and was engaged to be married. Conlin's mother was Emily's daughter and was at this time in poor health. Police in the surrounding area were alerted to be on the lookout for Conlin. He was arrested at Darlington on Sunday and taken to Stockton police station.

The Kirbys had a large family and were well known and popular; also, given the nature of their untimely deaths, it was no surprise that dense crowds lined the streets on the day of the funeral. On Thursday 27 September, the cortege left from Emily Kirby's son's house in Buchanan Street via Dovecot Street, High Street, Bridge Road and Thornaby Road to St Paul's church for a service; and then to Thornaby Cemetery for internment.

After initial hearings at Stockton police court Conlin was committed to stand trial at Newcastle Assizes. The case began on Friday 15 November before Justice Roche with CF Lowenthal and CP Scott acting for the prosecution and GB Sykes for the defence. The police had searched the Kirby's bungalow and found no evidence of foul play but the couple's breakfast had been prepared and not eaten. Emily's sister, Mary Jane Garbutt, had visited the couple on Saturday evening and had left at about 7.45. After this time whatever had actually taken place was witnessed solely by the murderer and the victims. The events could only be pieced together with the evidence that was available from fifty-eight witnesses heard over the two-day trial. Although circumstantial, the evidence was to form the unbroken links to a chain that was to wrap itself tightly around Conlin to prove he was guilty of the cold and calculated murder of his grandmother and her husband.

Two years previously, Conlin had worked for his grandmother, which would have given him an insight into her movements and habits. His wages from his part-time job were very low and it was known that he was short of money. On 18 September,

The village of Norton near to where Thomas and Emily Kirby were buried alive.
Author's collection

he had only collected £3 7s (£3.35p). There was a further £1 3s 8d (£1.18p) due to him but it was never collected. On Friday 21 September, he was at the working men's club in Norton that he frequented where he usually played dominoes. When asked to join in a game Conlin said he had no money and he told a man he owed money to that he would pay him later.

Conlin's bed had not been slept in on the Friday night and had been seen boarding an omnibus about two miles from Briargarth at 5.30 am on Saturday morning. He was then seen at about 6.20 am crossing a field carrying a spade and returning a little later empty handed. When a neighbour asked him what he was doing out at that time of the morning, Conlin had replied that he had been walking round Norton because he had not been to bed. That same morning he paid Doris, his sister, £28 10s (£28.50p) that he owed to her. She told the court that a poker had gone missing from her house and she had not seen it since. On waste land at Norton Avenue a small red car was often left by its owner. Between 3 and 5 am on Saturday this car was seen being driven from Norton towards Thornaby and, although the driver was not recognised by the witnesses, it was ascertained that it was not the owner. The car was later found abandoned not far from Briargarth.

William Brown, a tripe merchant from Buchanan Street, Stockton was Emily's son from her previous marriage and had often assisted her on the market stall. When he arrived at the market on Saturday morning and the couple were not there he went to their house but it was locked up. Brown then went to tell Conlin they were missing and asked him to help search for them. Conlin said he would take Brown's lorry and look for the couple. He then changed his clothes and drove the lorry to Darlington where it was later found abandoned. In Darlington, Conlin had purchased a pair of shoes, a suit and various other things. He then bought a second-hand motorcycle for £21 10s (£21.50p) in the name of Charles Murphy. Later that day Conlin met a young lady, Rose Mary McIntyre, to whom he also introduced himself as Charles Murphy. They made arrangements to meet up again that evening to go to a fair that was being held at Northallerton where he bought her a pair of silk stockings and other gifts. Meeting up again on Sunday morning, they went for a motorcycle ride to Richmond. On the return trip the motorcycle broke down at Barton so they completed the journey by bus. When they arrived back in Darlington they

A general view of the town of Richmond where William Conlin went for a ride on his motorcycle after having killed Emily and Thomas in 1928. Author's collection

went into St Cuthbert's church for a few minutes. As they left the church and were walking up Conniscliffe Road a policeman stopped them and asked their names. Conlin gave his name as Murphy but the policeman had a description of Conlin and was sure this was he so took him into custody. At the police station Conlin was searched and in his pocket a wallet containing more than £19 was found. On being questioned Conlin was in a state of collapse and said he could not remember anything, not even being in Darlington. In fact, he was so ill, that he was not fit to attend the initial hearing.

When the clothes Conlin had changed from on the Saturday morning were retrieved from his house and sent for examination a large smear of what proved to be a recent bloodstain was found. A grey hair matching that of Thomas was found on a trilby and on the trousers a hair matching that of Emily. In the pocket of Conlin's coat was fur that matched a coat belonging to Emily. It was concluded that the injuries to the couple could have been caused by a poker and the flat side of a spade. How they had been lured to the place of their murder was uncertain, perhaps with news of deterioration in Conlin's mother health,

The old church of St Cuthbert in Darlington where Conlin paid a visit prior to his arrest. The author

or an offer of an early morning lift to work. The other possibility was that he had attacked the couple in their home and then driven them to the field. He had been seen on an omnibus at 5.30 am coming from the direction of the Kirby's home on Saturday morning. Had he gone back to Briargarth to clean up any mess that was left? What seemed fairly certain was that after the deed he had abandoned the car then gone back to the street where he lived and taken a spade from a neighbour's coalhouse. There was a mark on the back of Emily's head that was consistent with the mark of being hit with a spade so when Conlin returned to the field to bury his grandparents had she regained consciousness necessitating the need to hit her again?

The most damning evidence of all was that Conlin could not account for the money he had spent and been found with and testimony from Ernest Vickers, Emily's son-in-law and Thomas Kirby junior who both identified the wallet that had been in Conlin's possession as the one given as a wedding present at the Kirby's marriage. A plea of insanity was brought by the defence as Conlin stated that he could not remember any of the events that took place from the Friday until the

A photo published at the time of the murders of Thomas and Emily Kirby in happier times. Northern Daily Gazette

Sunday of his arrest. There was no evidence, medical or otherwise to substantiate this claim.

The jury were absent for three-quarters of an hour before returning a verdict of guilty of wilful murder. Conlin's female relatives and Miss Lofthouse, his fiancée, left the court before the verdict was given, either in disgust or not wanting to hear the final sentence. Conlin stood in the dock dressed in a smart suit which had been purchased with blood money. He was pale and fidgety as Justice Roche donned the black cap and sentenced him to death. The plea of insanity was taken to the Criminal Court of Appeal but no reprieve was granted.

A grey dawn broke over the City of Durham on Friday 4 January 1929 as Thomas Pierrepoint made his way to the condemned cell to prepare Conlin for his execution. The small crowd gathered outside the gaol consisted mainly of women who stood with heads bowed. The few men that were present removed their hats as the cathedral clock chimed eight. They all read the notice that declared justice had been served before drifting away to carry out their normal daily routine.

Not Suicide, 1929
James Johnson, his wife, Mary Ann, and their four children lived at 68 Cannon Street, Elswick. Forty-three-year-old Johnson, who was crippled, worked as a bookmaker. He was well known to the police for various offences including theft, assault, being drunk and disorderly, and had served time in prison on a few occasions. At the end of March in 1929, when Johnson was released after completing a sixty day sentence, he heard rumours that his wife had been having an affair with a man named Billy Ridley. Mary denied the stories but two of their children, thirteen-year-old Nancy and eight-year-old Jenny, told their dad that their mother had been seeing another man. This caused mounting arguments between the couple and, on Thursday 9 May, Mary went to the police to complain about her husband's behaviour. PC George Thomas Urwin went to speak to James who told him that Mary's behaviour was not squeaky clean either as she had hit him with a rolling pin. Mary then reached into her husband's pocket and pulled out a razor telling Urwin that James had said he was keeping it for her.

The following day the Johnson's youngest child, Irene, became ill and was taken to hospital so was not in the house when the situation between the couple must have spiralled out of control.

On 11 May, Mary had visited her mother and left to return home with the other three children at about 11 pm. At about 1 am on Sunday 12 May Thomas Held, who lived in the room next to the family, became concerned when he heard a suspicious bump followed by a moan. He called on another neighbour and the two men knocked on the Johnson's door. There was no reply but there was a smell of gas so they forced the door open. On entering the men discovered their concerns were well founded as gas poured out from the unlit jets of the cooker. They turned off the gas at the tap and went for the police.

Nancy, Jenny and five-year-old James were suffering from the effects of the fumes but they all later recovered. Mary was not so lucky, her throat had been cut. Johnson was lying in another room also suffering from the effects of the poisonous substance. His hands were covered in blood. The police arrested and charged him with murder.

His trial was held at Newcastle Assizes on Tuesday 2 July before Justice Robert Bannatyne Finlay with Arthur Morley acting for the prosecution and RF Burnand for the defence.

Johnson's version of events was that Mary had committed suicide by turning the gas on and then cutting her own throat but his bloodstained hands had given him away and medical opinion was that it was highly unlikely that the wound to Mary's throat could have been self inflicted. There was also evidence from PC Urwin, neighbours and family that told of a violent troubled relationship between the couple.

After a trial lasting two days, Johnson was found guilty and hanged by Thomas Pierrepoint on Wednesday 7 August 1929.

CHAPTER 22

Evidence of Insanity
1933

Ernest Wadge Parker, along with his twin brother Sydney, ran a small family fruit and vegetable business at West Stanley. Thomas, their father, and Lily, their sister, did not see eye to eye with Parker and there were constant arguments. The situation became steadily worse towards the end of 1932 and the police were called on numerous occasions because Parker had assaulted his father and sister.

In April 1933, Parker was given a two month custodial sentence for yet another assault on Lily. He was released on 17 June and made straight for 3 Blooms Avenue where the family lived. They did not want him there and he was told to stay away. This must have added fuel to the already smouldering fire as Parker told an acquaintance, James Calvert, that he was going to kill his father and sister.

Early on the morning of Sunday 25 June, Parker went to the house again and when his father refused him entry he smashed a window and climbed in. His father tried to make him leave but Ernest launched another assault and when Lily became involved he hit her in the face. The police were called and managed to evict Parker but he was not to be got rid of so easily and returned at about 1 pm. Once again the police were called to escort him from the premises.

The family must have thought they had seen the last of Parker for that day at least so, at about 3 pm, Thomas went out leaving Lily in the house with her twelve-year-old daughter, Elsie May. Elsie was in another room when she heard a commotion. On going to investigate she saw Parker attacking her mother with an axe, a sight that must have given her nightmares for the rest of her life. She ran out screaming and PC Thomas

Newcastle Infirmary where Lily Parker died after having been shot by her brother.
Author's collection

Lindsay, who was nearby, returned to the house with Elsie. Parker offered no resistance and was arrested. Thirty-six year old Lily was rushed to the Newcastle infirmary where she died later that evening. Parker showed no remorse for his act and, in fact, told the police he was glad Lily was dead and that she had deserved it.

The chimes of the Durham Cathedral clock rang out the hour as Ernest Parker was hanged in 1933. Author's collection

His trial was held at Durham Assizes on 14 November before Justice Humphreys with W Hedley and Mr Covingham for the prosecution and JW Jardine and J Harvey Robson for the defence. A plea of insanity was brought by the defence as from August 1916 to February 1917 Parker had been confined as an inmate in the Durham County Mental Hospital. His mother had also been in the same hospital for two years and had died there in 1914 when Parker was just six. The jury ignored the plea and brought in a verdict of guilty to wilful murder.

Parker was hanged on Wednesday 6 December 1933 by Thomas Pierrepoint. About a dozen people had gathered outside the prison and as the Durham Cathedral chimes were striking the hour of eight they removed their hats and bowed their heads. The small crowd did not include anyone from Parker's home town of West Stanley.

CHAPTER 23

Blood Money
1935

Edward Frederick Herdman was born in Morpeth and had moved to Bishop Auckland in about 1905. In 1934 he was aged seventy-five and worked as a solicitor's clerk to Messrs J Jenning and Son. Herdman was well known in County Durham as a historian and a collector of rare coins and communion tokens and also an upstanding member of the Tenter Street Methodist church. He had two sons and a daughter living within the area and another daughter, Jane, who lived with him at Salisbury Place.

On New Years Eve 1934, Jane returned to her father's house shortly before 10 pm. She knocked on the door to be let in but there was no reply. After waiting a short time she walked around the outside of the house, and, finding the sitting room window unlatched, climbed through. On entering the dining room the reason there had been no answer to Jane's knock became all too clear. Her father was lying on the floor with his head under the table. There were obvious signs of a struggle as the furniture was in disarray and there was blood everywhere, even on the walls. On the table was a bloodstained brass poker with the head broken off and Herdman's wallet. Jane immediately went to see to her father but it was too late to do anything for him. He had terrible injuries to his head and his throat was cut. Lying on the lapel of his jacket was his own pocket knife which was open. Herdman's wallet, which he usually carried in the inside pocket of his jacket, contained £40. There was also money in the dead man's pocket and £58.10s (£58.50) in the desk. A doctor conducted a medical examination of the body at 10.20 pm which showed that Herdman's jugular vein had been severed and that he had also sustained a fractured skull. It was thought that he had been dead about two to two and a half hours.

Jane Herdman gave information to the Bishop Auckland police, which led them to suspect John Stephenson Bainbridge, a twenty-six-year-old private in the 1st Battalion, Durham Light Infantry. He lived with his widowed mother in the same street as Herdman and the two men had worked together at the solicitor's office until Bainbridge had joined the army. He had been stationed for some time at Blackdown Camp in Surrey and had returned to Bishop Auckland on leave on 22 December.

After police investigations had been carried out Bainbridge was arrested and charged with robbery and murder.

What was to be a four day trial began at Durham Assizes on Monday 4 March 1935 before Justice Goddard with CP Scott and J Charlesworth acting for the prosecution and GR Vick and JH Robson for the defence.

It transpired that Bainbridge had been to a money-lender and borrowed two sums, the bulk of which had not been repaid. At the beginning of December he had tried to borrow a further £20 but he was refused.

Bainbridge had been courting Helen Wright who worked as a buffet maid at the *Queen's Hotel* in Gateshead. In November he had bought an engagement ring in a shop at Bishop Auckland. The jeweller, Mr Hornsby, took a deposit and let Bainbridge take the ring on the promise of the balance later but the ring was not the right size so it was returned to

Men of the Durham Light Infantry to which regiment John Bainbridge belonged. Author's collection

the shop. Mr Hornsby decided not to let him have another until he could pay the remaining balance.

Bainbridge had come home on leave with a friend, Joseph McNally, and they were supposed to return to their unit on 2 January. On New Year's Eve, he had visited his fiancée at Gateshead and then returned to Bishop Auckland by bus arranging to meet Helen later. He then visited the jeweller's shop and said he would return that evening to pay for the ring. Bainbridge had then called to see Herdman at about 5.20 pm but he was not at home. He told Jane he wished to discuss his will with her father so she invited him to wait. Herdman returned at about 6.10 pm and the two men sat in the study talking until 7.45 pm when Bainbridge and Jane left the house together. At 8.10 pm a witness had seen Bainbridge as he walked up the back lane that led to Herdman's house. At 8.15 pm he was seen by another witness in Newgate Street. At about 8.20 pm Bainbridge went back to the jeweller's shop and paid the balance on the ring with three £1 notes. Just before 10 pm he was at the *Queen's Hotel*, where, it was said, he spent money fairly freely. From about 11 pm to 1.30 am he was at a New Year's Eve party at Helen's house.

In the days before home entertainment systems were commonplace a musical instrument being played or party games would help the event to be successful. This party was no exception and amongst the games was one called Buttons, which involved the men undoing their buttons one by one until stripped to the waist. Another was called Murder, which involved cutting a pack of cards. Bainbridge ended up with the Ace of Spades, which meant he could be cross-examined by the other players as a murderer. He played his part in these games with no show of embarrassment and no hint to show that he may have committed a real murder shortly before arriving at the party. While he was at the house he made a will telling Helen it was because he may be sent abroad to fight with his unit.

On Thursday 3 January, McNally, who had arrived back at Blackdown Camp, received an envelope containing £36 in folded notes, some in sequence and a few which were bloodstained. Knowing about the murder, McNally handed the envelope, postmarked in Gateshead, and money to the police.

There was no letter included but it was thought that the handwriting on the envelope matched that of the will that Bainbridge had written. One of the notes that was in the till at the *Queen's Hotel* matched the sequence of notes that were sent to McNally, although no one could say for sure who paid with that particular note.

A letter was produced in court that had been sent in reply to the moneylender's request for payment of what was owed to him by Bainbridge. The letter was signed with Bainbridge's name and stated that a Bishop Auckland solicitor had been very helpful to him and he was hoping to soon have a job as an army teacher and to be on better wages. Where usually he had to appeal to his mother for financial help he was hoping not to have to cadge from her in the future.

> *In fact, I will receive such a large sum as will seem to me to be that of a millionaire, and with this solicitor behind me, there is but little doubt of my success. My mother will pay you something every month now and if there are any arrears I shall be able to wipe them off in a short time. Mother will send each month as much as she possibly can and whatever remains I will be responsible for.*

Newgate Street, Bishop Auckland where John Bainbridge was seen by a witness on the night of the murder. Author's collection

Jane Herdman testified that she and Bainbridge's family were close friends. She knew of no one who had any motive to kill her father. Jane thought that Bainbridge would have known that her father would have a considerable amount of money on his person and in his study but she did not know exactly how much was missing. Herdman received his wages in consecutive notes and the notes that were sent to McNally were in sequence although the notes with which Bainbridge had paid for the ring were not.

When Bainbridge was arrested the only sign of blood on his person was a small spot on his shirt sleeve that he said came from a shaving cut. It was generally agreed that after slashing someone's throat and then beating them about the head with a poker the assailant should have been splashed with blood. Bainbridge had been at a party stripped to the waist a few hours after the crime with no traces of blood to be seen on his body or his clothes. Those that attended the party said that Bainbridge had shown no sign of guilt or embarrassment whilst they were in his company.

A handwriting expert who had inspected the will, the letter and the envelope produced in evidence could not say beyond a doubt that the writer of all three was the same although there were similarities. The time factor was important, in fact the case became known as the 'ten minute alibi'. The prosecution stated that Herdman had been murdered at about 8.10 pm. Bainbridge had been seen by witnesses from 8.10 pm onwards that evening. If he had committed the murder he would have had to have done so in double quick time and then cleaned himself of any blood before the first witness had seen him.

Bainbridge pleaded not guilty to both murder and robbery. He testified that before he had met Helen Wright he had had an affair with a married woman. The money he had used to pay for the ring had been borrowed from her. When asked who the woman was, Bainbridge refused to disclose her identity. He told the police and the court that it would put her in a compromising position with her husband and he did not wish to cause her any problems or distress.

There appeared to be no motive for the brutal murder except robbery. The prosecution put forward the argument that the money was left behind at the scene because the perpetrator had got cold feet and thought that if he remained any longer he would be discovered. The evidence against Bainbridge was his spending on New Year's Eve, the money that had been sent to McNally from a post-box in Gateshead and the fact that he had paid for the ring. There was also the fact that some of the notes were in sequence and matched with the note from the till at the hotel where Bainbridge had bought drinks. It was suggested that he had sent the money to McNally because if it had been found on him he could have not possibly explained how it had come into his possession.

Justice Goddard told Bainbridge that if he would not disclose the identity of the person from whom he had obtained the money the outcome of the trial would be against him.

Although there was only a ten minute window in which Bainbridge could have committed the crime the jury felt that the evidence was enough to bring in a verdict of guilty of wilful murder. His defence appealed but the House of Lords backed the original decision and would not grant even a postponement of the execution.

Before the death sentence was due to be carried out Bainbridge's mother received a letter signed 'a great friend' claiming to be the woman that had lent him the money and saying that he was innocent.

Mrs Violet Van der Elst, a tireless campaigner against the death penalty, led demonstrations, sent telegrams to the King and Queen and offered a reward of £350 for the mystery woman to come forward, to try and keep the young man from facing the rope. All her efforts were in vain and Bainbridge was hanged on Thursday 9 May 1935 by Thomas Pierrepoint while the rest of Britain celebrated the Silver Jubilee of King George V.

A Silver Jubilee Celebration, 1935

Amanda Sharp was twenty and worked as a kitchen maid at Langley Park Fever Hospital. For about six months, she had been seeing twenty-three-year-old George Hague. Since October of 1934 Hague had lodged with Mary and Robert Lodge, his sister and brother-in-law, at Cross Fell House in

The village of Langley Park, where George Hague lodged with his sister and her husband. Author's collection

Langley Park. He usually worked as a bus conductor but in May 1935 he was unemployed.

On Monday 6 May, the Silver Jubilee celebrations for King George V were to be held at Ushaw College. Amongst other events there was to be a huge bonfire. The maids and some of the staff from the hospital were going to the party and late passes had been arranged for them which meant they could stay out until midnight. Amanda had decided to go with her co-workers rather than her boyfriend. Hague at first thought that the matron had told the maids that they could not go to the celebrations with their boyfriends but must go in a group with the other staff. On 5 May he found out that this was not so, and becoming very angry, he quarrelled with Amanda. Hague told her that if she preferred other company rather than his he would not see her any more.

On 6 May Hague tried to see Amanda several times to make up with her but she refused to talk to him. He eventually went to Amanda's parents' house at Garden Avenue but her mother told Hague to leave her daughter alone as she was finished with him. Hague, crying bitterly, had then said: 'Well no one will get her then.'

After the celebrations Amanda and her co-workers were walking up the drive to the hospital when a man startled them. Some of the nurses recognised the man as being Hague. He stopped Amanda so the rest of the group walked on thinking he just wanted to talk. One of the nurses, Mary Johnson, turned round a few seconds later to see Amanda on the ground with her throat cut.

Hague was arrested and after an initial hearing held at Consett Police Court he was ordered to stand trial at Durham on Friday 28 June before Justice du Parcq with JW Jardine for the prosecution and JF Robson for the defence.

Hague's defence put forward a plea of insanity and witnesses were called to substantiate the suggestion. Annie, Hague's mother said that he was the youngest of thirteen children and was born when she was forty-five. He was born at a time in her life when she was quarrelsome and bad tempered. He had a cousin that was an inmate of an asylum, an aunt who had died in a mental hospital and one of his brothers, John William Hague, had committed suicide. Dr B Crosthwaite of Houghton-le-Spring stated that children born under these circumstances were often paranoid. Dr James W Astley-Cooper, of Middleton Hall Private Mental Institution, stated that Hague was of unsound mind before, during and after the attack on Amanda. The doctor was of the opinion that Hague was suffering from paranoia and had no remorse or anxiety about what he had done. Hague thought that Amanda was the jealous one in the relationship when, in fact, it was he. Because of his paranoia he was shifting the blame. Dr TC Barkas, also of Middleton Hall, stated that, although it was not easy to detect paranoia in the early stages, Hague had a general indifference about him that one would not expect in a normal person after committing such a crime.

Dr GF Walker, consulting physician of the Sunderland Municipal Hospital, also gave evidence that Hague was in the early stages of paranoia. There was an air of unreality about him and he nursed grossly erroneous notions which he acted on from time to time. The prosecution pointed out that if Amanda

Ushaw College, where Amanda Sharp had attended the Silver Jubilee celebrations prior to her murder in 1935. Author's collection

had not died there would never have been any suggestion of Hague being insane. They submitted that Hague had taken a razor from his house, waited for Amanda and cut her throat with the intention of murder.

At the two-day trial the jury swept aside the evidence of the medical men and insanity as a defence and took just three-quarters of an hour to find Hague guilty of wilful murder. Justice du Parcq agreed with the decision and pronounced sentence of death.

An appeal was unsuccessful and Hague was hanged at 8 am on Tuesday 16 July 1935 by Thomas Pierrepoint. At 7.50 am members of the Society of St Vincent de Paul filed into St Cuthbert's church opposite the gaol to pray for the condemned man.

CHAPTER 24

Murdered by Her Nephew 1936

Mrs Harriet May Linney was a 'ready money' book-maker. Money that was paid in as stakes would consist of anything from coppers to silver coins. It was common for her to have anything between £5 and £20 overnight in her home at 1 Hetton Place in Sunderland where it would remain until the following day.

On Tuesday 30 June 1936, Harriet's husband, James, a retired bookmaker, was away all day in Carlisle. When he returned it was to find that his sixty-two-year-old wife had been robbed and murdered.

Mrs Hall, a neighbour, had seen a tall, strapping, young fellow knock on the door of number one at about 6 pm on the evening of 30 June. The man was wearing a green, felt hat and was carrying a mackintosh over his arm. Mrs Hall thought this rather odd as it was a very warm day. Harriet had opened the door and the man entered the house. That was the last time Harriet was seen alive.

At about eight o'clock that same evening another neighbour, Mrs Dunn, was walking past the Linney's house when she noticed the back door was standing open. Mrs Dunn went inside and found Harriet lying dead with her head resting on the fire grate. There were injuries to her head and her face was covered with blood. A doctor was called and he estimated Harriet had been dead for over an hour.

She had been struck first with fists. There were bruises to her face, three of her bottom teeth were knocked out and her upper denture was found on the floor some distance away. A blow to the front of the head had smashed in the skull and there were numerous other injuries which pointed to severe and repeated blows. There were also bruises to Harriet's arms consistent with trying to ward off her attacker. Near the body was a broken bottle and a bent poker which had been used to commit the brutal and violent murder. Every room in the house had been ransacked. Betting slips were strewn all over the floor and there was no money to be found.

Christopher Jackson was twenty-three and the Linney's nephew. He had been in the army at Catterick but had been discharged after spending six months in prison for breaking into a warehouse. For a few weeks prior to the murder Jackson had been lodging at the house of Mrs Bainbridge at 23 Front Street, Chester-le-Street. Jackson had been living at King Street in Rotherham when he met Mrs Bainbridge's son and had then travelled up to Chester-le-Street with him to stay with his family. Jackson had not paid his rent to Mrs Bainbridge for three weeks and had borrowed money from her son and daughter. On the morning of 30 June he had told his landlady that he was owed six guineas (£6.60) from Catterick and asked her to lend him 2s (10p). Mrs Bainbridge had no money but asked her insurance agent for a loan. The agent gave her half a crown (26p) which she handed to Jackson. He left the house and returned about an hour later wearing the mackintosh buttoned up to the neck. Jackson took a suitcase from under his bed and then said he was going to have a bath. After his bath he paid Mrs Bainbridge the money he owed her for lodge and the insurance agent and also paid the money he owed to her son and daughter.

When the police began to investigate the murder they found out that Jackson fitted the description given by Mrs Hall of the man seen at the Linney's door. They then found that he had a record of stealing from when he was nine years old. They asked James Linney if he knew about his nephew's record and he said he did. Linney said that he had felt sorry for him and had helped him out with money on several occasions.

The police went to Jackson's lodgings and took him to the police station to question him. The suitcase, which was locked, was also taken. When he was asked for the key, Jackson said he had thrown it away so the police broke the case open. In it was Jackson's bloodstained suit. There were bits of glass in the turn-ups of the trousers which matched the broken bottle found at the scene of the crime. There was also money tied up in a handkerchief, all in coppers and silver. Jackson was charged with the murder of his aunt.

Jackson's trial was held at Durham Assizes on Wednesday 4 November before Justice Goddard with CP Scott and Herbert RB Shepherd acting for the prosecution and HIB Hallet and JH Robson for the defence. Jackson said his aunt had provoked him and he had gone to the house hoping his uncle would help him with money as he had done so in the past. Apparently his aunt was not so soft because when Jackson told her what he had come for and asked if he could wait for his uncle's return, she refused. According to Jackson, his aunt called him names and tried to push him out of the house. She had a poker in her hand and struck him with it three times and then had attacked him with a flat iron. Jackson then pushed her against a table and hit her with a bottle. After that he could remember nothing. He said he completely lost his temper and did not remember hitting Harriet with the poker or ransacking the house. He did, however, remember picking up the money. Jackson said he had no intention of robbery or killing his aunt when he went to the house. Medical examination showed bruising on Jackson which seemed to verify his statement that he had been hit with an iron and perhaps punched.

Paley Scott, for the prosecution, did not finish his cross-examination and in his summing up to the jury he stated it was because Jackson's evidence was impossible to believe. If there was no intention of robbery or murder, why then was he carrying a mackintosh on a hot day? It was to cover his clothing in case they became bloodstained.

According to the medical evidence, terrible violence had been used to murder Harriet and it must be obvious that this was intentional. The jury agreed with the prosecution and Jackson was found guilty. Before passing the death sentence the judge addressed Jackson, saying: 'I can hold out no hope for you that the sentence I am about to pass will not be carried out.'

Christopher Jackson was hanged on Wednesday 16 December 1936 by Thomas Pierrepoint.

CHAPTER 25

Guilty until Proven Innocent!
1938

Many of the cases related in this publication went to trial with the accused convicted on extremely flimsy evidence by present standards. The arrest, trial, conviction and subsequent execution of Robert William Hoolhouse must be the most controversial of them all.

In January 1938, Hoolhouse was twenty-one although his mental age was considered younger, perhaps by about seven years. He usually worked as a farm labourer but things were quiet over the winter months and at the time of these events he was unemployed. He and his father had worked for Henry and Margaret Jane Dobson at High Grange Farm at Wolviston but in 1933 there had been a dispute between Mr Hoolhouse and his employer which resulted in the loss of their jobs.

The village of Wolviston where the Hoolhouse family had lived and worked at High Grange Farm up until 1933. Author's collection

The family were evicted from their tied cottage and went to live at 6 Pickering Street in Haverton Hill. This must have had a devastating impact at the time but it was nothing compared to the link that would be forged with this and the tragic event that was to take place five years later.

On Tuesday 18 January 1938, sixty-seven-year-old Margaret Dobson had left the farm in mid-afternoon and did not return home. There had been no cause for alarm as it was assumed she had stayed overnight with her daughter in Newcastle. On the following morning her husband, Henry, was walking to Wolviston when he saw something in a ploughed field just off the main North Stockton road near to the lane leading to High Grange Farm. On closer inspection, with disbelief and horror, he discovered it was the body of his wife. On a post-mortem being carried out it was ascertained that Margaret had died from shock following injuries that had been inflicted upon her. She had been brutally raped and had sustained two stab wounds. An examination of the stomach contents of the victim put her death sometime before 4 pm the previous day.

The sacking and eviction of the Hoolhouse family from the farm was common knowledge and the police concluded that this could be seen as a strong motive for murder. It then came to their attention that Hoolhouse had been seen with scratches on his face. They went to his house in the early hours of Thursday morning and, telling him to get dressed, took him into custody. Bloodstains were noticed on his clothes and Hoolhouse was questioned as to his whereabouts on Tuesday afternoon and he gave a detailed statement.

Hoolhouse said that he had left home about 12.30 pm and cycled to Wolviston. He was in the company of William Husband, John Lax and his sister Dolly until 3.30 pm, arriving home again at about 4 pm. Hoolhouse had arranged to return to pick Dolly up that evening to take her to the pictures. He caught a bus at 6.30 that evening where he talked to a postman he knew until he arrived at his stop. Hoolhouse took Dolly to the pictures at Billingham that evening and then put her on the bus to her home at 11 pm before catching his own bus home. The following day he left his house to sign on at the Labour Exchange at about 11 am then cycled back to Wolviston to see

Husband where he stayed until mid-afternoon. On the way to Wolviston he said he had fallen of his bicycle and that was how he had sustained the scratches to his face. The bloodstains on his clothes he explained by saying they were from the scratches and spots that were on his shirt cuff were from cutting himself while shaving.

On Husband and the Lax's being questioned they gave the time of their friend's departure on Tuesday afternoon as nearly an hour later. Hoolhouse answer to this was that he had merely made a mistake with the time and must have arrived home at 5 pm not 4 pm as he had thought. The discrepancy in the time gave the police all the proof they needed to come to the conclusion that the missing hour was when Hoolhouse was attacking his victim and was committed to stand trial for rape and wilful murder.

Hoolhouse's trial began at Leeds on 28 March before Justice Wrottesley with AP Peaker and CP Scott for the prosecution and A Morley and WA MacFarlane for the defence with the whole case seeming to be resting on Hoolhouse being guilty until proven innocent instead of the other way around.

The case by the prosecution rested on Hoolhouse having a motive and also the time factor and police evidence that stated Hoolhouse had deliberately lied in his statement about where he was at the time of the murder and the physical evidence of the scratches on his face and bloodstained clothes.

The defence pointed out that when the police made the arrest Hoolhouse donned the same clothes that he had been wearing on that Tuesday. If he had been guilty surely he would have not brought the attention of the police to bloodstains by wearing the clothes in which he had committed a murder. The blood had been tested and found to be the same group as Mrs Dobson's but it was also the same blood group shared by forty percent of the population. Hoolhouse was asked to take a blood test but declined. Even if he had taken the test and had been the same group, which was highly likely, this would not have helped the investigation. No traces of semen were found on his clothes although the victim had been raped. Near to the body a rather indeterminate footprint had been found underneath the prints of Margaret's husband's boots. The clay in the field was crumbly because of the recent ploughing. A plaster cast of the print had been made and it was compared to Hoolhouse's boots and, although it was found to be similar it did not have the distinguishing marks on the soles. The prosecution agreed that the print could not be used as evidence against Hoolhouse.

Percy Swales had seen a man at 5.30 pm in the vicinity of the scene of the crime. Swales had been some distance away but described the man as having Hoolhouse's build and wearing leggings. It was established that Hoolhouse did not possess leggings so it was probable that the man seen was the perpetrator and that the time of death given was wrong and the victim had died nearer 5 pm. By that time Hoolhouse was definitely at home. The postman that he had spoken to on the bus, John and Dolly Lax and William Husband all said there was nothing unusual in his manner later that evening. Certainly there was nothing to show that he may have committed a murder shortly beforehand.

Much was made by Justice Wrottesley on Hoolhouse's change of statement and very little on evidence that showed doubt which perhaps swayed the jury towards their final verdict. On Monday 30 March, after four hours debate, the jury brought in a verdict of guilty against Hoolhouse.

On Monday 9 May an appeal was heard before Justices du Parcq, Branson and Humphreys but it was denied, again on the evidence of the police relating to the discrepancy of the time. Also denied was a petition for a reprieve consisting of 14,000 names including those of nine northern MPs. No one ever looked for the mysterious man that had been seen in the field that fateful day and Robert Hoolhouse was hanged by Thomas Pierrepoint on Thursday 26 May 1938.

Hundreds of people gathered outside the gaol, led in a demonstration by Violet Van der Elst. Although the abolition of capital punishment in Britain was still many years into the future this case caused a strong argument for the voices of the protesters to be heard.

Suffer the Children, 1938
William Parker lived with his wife, Jane Ann, and their two children, Theresa, aged thirteen months, and Cecil, two months,

at 23 Edwin Street, Newcastle. On Monday 25 April, Parker walked into a police station and told the officers on duty that he had killed his wife at their house on 22 April. He said he had been walking the streets since then not knowing what to do. The police went to the house and found the bodies of Jane and the two children with string tied tightly around their necks. Strangulation appeared to have been the cause of death for all three but Jane had also sustained a severe battering which may have killed her before she was strangled. Parker admitted to the murder of his wife but denied having killed his children. He was committed to stand trial charged with all three murders.

Parker stood at Durham Assizes on Thursday 16 June before Justice Atkinson with GR Vick and Norman Harper acting for the prosecution and Clifford Cohen and G Streatfield for the defence. Parker's version of what had taken place was that he had arrived home to find his wife with her hands round the throat of their son. Asking her what she was doing Jane told him that he was too late. Parker then realized that both his children were dead and that his wife had strangled them with string. Jane then lifted up a poker and ran at him with it. Parker ran into the scullery and Jane followed. He picked up a hammer, the nearest object to hand, and battered his wife to death. In an act of revenge for what Jane had done to the children, Parker tied a piece of string around her neck and then left the house.

Parker's sisters were in court and stated that a neighbour, Hildreth King, had said that Jane had told her she had money worries and had thought of killing her children and then herself. When the neighbour was questioned she denied that she had told anyone of such a conversation and said it had never taken place. If Parker's version of events had been believed then he could only have been found guilty of manslaughter because of extreme provocation. The jury did not accept his story and brought in a verdict of guilty of wilful murder and sentence of death was passed. Parker was hanged on Tuesday 26 July 1938 by Thomas Pierrepoint.

CHAPTER 26

Robbery and Murder at Wigton
1939

James Irwin Percival, his wife, Mary and their two grown children, James and Kate, lived at Aikhead Farm near Wigton. Percival had farmed the 120 acres of land for about thirty years and, during busy times such as harvesting, help would be hired on a temporary basis. One of the men that Percival employed was John Daymond, a nineteen-year-old farm labourer originally from North Side, Workington. His father was dead and his mother in service. When Daymond was working on a farm he would sleep in a loft or a barn but when he had no employment he was of no fixed abode.

On Wednesday 9 November 1938, Percival, as was his habit, left the house early to feed the calves. His daughter was sitting in the farmhouse reading a letter between 7 and 8 am when she heard sounds of a struggle outside. On going to investigate, Kate found her father and brother, both lying on the floor of the engine-house, unconscious and bleeding. Kate went to the adjoining farm for help from their neighbour, Edwin Mann. Between them they managed to carry the two men into the farmhouse and the police were sent for. James junior recovered enough to tell Mann that he had heard his father shout for help and, on going to his assistance, was himself struck from behind. All he could remember at that time was seeing a man in a dark coat. When the police and medical help arrived, both father and son were taken to Carlisle infirmary with severe head injuries. Percival died the following afternoon and James junior remained in a critical condition.

When the police searched the outbuildings they found Daymond sleeping under some straw in the barn. When he was aroused he said that he had been there all night but on further questioning as to what had occurred Daymond stated that he had 'hit the old man and then the son'. The police asked him what he had used and Daymond pointed to a bloodstained pick-axe hanging on the wall. He was arrested and taken to Wigton Police Station. On his pockets being searched he was found to have a shilling, eighteen pennies and five halfpennies (approximately 30p) of which only one halfpenny was his. Daymond had acquired the remainder of the money by rifling the pockets of his unconscious victims.

The following day, when Percival died, Daymond was charged with murder and of the wounding with intent to murder of James junior. After initial inquests at Wigton Police Court he was committed to stand trial at the Cumberland Assizes. Daymond pleaded not guilty even though he had admitted to the police that he was responsible.

The trial began at Carlisle on Thursday 19 January 1939 before Justice Croom-Johnson with CTB Leigh and WH Openshaw for the prosecution and Selwyn Lloyd and NB Birrell for the defence. Police enquiries had revealed that Daymond had lost his job on 7 November and was in debt. Because he had worked at Aikhead Farm he would have known Percival's movements and that he sometimes had large amounts of money on his person. When Dr JS Faulds, pathologist, was questioned as to the injuries on the dead man he stated that there had been five blows to the head using considerable force. In his opinion these blows had been inflicted with the pickaxe that had been found by the police. All the wounds had been severe causing multiple fractures of the skull. When Daymond was arrested his clothes showed no signs of bloodstains. The pathologist explained that the two victims were wearing caps which would have prevented the blood spraying onto the assailant. Dr Meldrum then reported on James junior's condition. He had received one blow to the head and, although he was improving physically, his mental condition remained impaired. James junior was not fit enough to appear in court but he had signed a statement that said he now remembered that the man he had seen in the dark coat was Daymond.

Daymond's defence put forward a plea of insanity as it was stated that there had been mental illness on both sides of his family and he could have inherited these traits. There had been a full moon on 7 November, two days before the attack, and it was believed that insanity could come to the fore during this time. Dr BG Derry, medical officer of Durham Gaol, stated that this was a primitive belief and there was no evidence at all to suggest it being true. He added that he had kept Daymond under constant observation and, in his opinion, the prisoner was of sound mind.

The prosecution pointed out that all the evidence pointed to a cold, calculated attack on Daymond's two victims. Since the crime he had shown no remorse and seemed indifferent to the consequences of his actions. After retiring for just over an hour the jury returned a verdict of guilty of murder in the furtherance of theft but with a recommendation to mercy because of his youth. A petition was signed with over 5,000 names but no reprieve was granted and a young man, in the prime of his life, was hanged by Thomas Pierrepoint on Wednesday 8 February 1939.

CHAPTER 27

Murder of a Policeman 1940

In the early hours of the morning of Thursday 29 February 1940, a tragic event rocked the usually peaceful village of Coxhoe. Jesse Smith was cycling past the Co-operative store when he saw a light inside. This being unusual, he reported it to the police. A police constable of the Durham constabulary, William Ralph Shiell, was on duty with War Reserve William Stafford when they were alerted to the cyclist's suspicions that the store was being robbed. On the three men going to investigate they noticed that a bolt had been withdrawn on the back gate. Shiell went to the front of the store and Stafford and Smith tried to gain entrance from the rear. It is believed that the intruders must have heard Stafford trying to get in and they made a dash straight through a plate glass window and ran off into the darkness. Shiell was nearest to the window when the two men appeared and he immediately gave chase. Stafford and Smith had heard the glass smashing and the sound of running feet so they also gave chase but were some distance behind. The culprits ran down the main street and crossed the road onto some waste ground behind Long Row. The sound of running feet stopped and Stafford and Smith did not know where the three men had gone. They spent some time searching and eventually found Shiell lying on the waste ground badly wounded. Two miners on their way to work stopped to help Stafford carry his colleague to a nearby house which was number 53 Long Row. When Robert Sanderson opened his door to a loud knocking at 2.15 am it was to see Shiell lying on the pavement. The four men carried him into the kitchen and laid him on a mat in front of the fire. Shiell was bleeding from a wound in his lower right side but was conscious and asked for a cigarette and a glass of water which he was given. When a doctor had attended he was taken to the Durham County Hospital where he died the following morning. Before Shiell died he was able to make a statement to his senior officers. He said there were two men and as he was catching up to them he had heard one of the men tell the other to 'let him have it'. He was able to give further information, including a description of one of the men, and, along with evidence that was found in the store, the police had plenty to follow up on. A reward of £50 was offered for information leading to an arrest.

Shiell, who was twenty-eight, left behind a wife and a five-year-old daughter.

When the police searched the Co-operative store it was found that the intruders had gained entrance through a skylight. There was little missing from the store, probably because the thieves had been disturbed, but there was damage to goods from the broken window. The marks of a new car tyre were found in a lane nearby so police made enquiries at garages throughout the North East, especially in Tynemouth. A car, which had been stolen from Chester-le-Street, was found partially burnt

The village of Coxhoe where William Shiell of the Durham Constabulary was shot and killed in 1940. Author's collection

out and, on a comparison made, the tyres were found to match those near the scene of the crime.

On 5 March, two men from Hawkesworth were arrested in Otley. They were William Appleby who was twenty-seven and Vincent Ostler who was twenty-four. They were charged with the murder of PC Shiell and remanded to Durham Gaol.

The trial before Justice Hilbery at Leeds Assizes began on Monday 6 May with R Vick and Dennis Robson acting for the prosecution and CP Scott, JW Jardine, JS Snowden and Willard Sexton for the defence. Appleby gave evidence in his own defence and mentioned numerous burglaries he said he had committed with Ostler. He would have believed that these confessions would have helped his case but in this he was mistaken. According to Shiell's description in his dying statement one man had shouted 'Let him have it' and the other had fired the shot. The jury were instructed by Justice Hilbery not to let their minds be prejudiced or influenced by these revelations of past offences. Whether the outcome of the trial meant that the jury had not heeded the court's directions only those twelve people sitting in judgement knew. After a trial lasting four days, both men were found guilty of wilful murder but with a recommendation of mercy for Appleby.

An appeal was launched by both men. Ostler's argument was that there was no direct evidence as to which of the two men had fired the fatal shot. Appleby's appeal was based on misdirection to the jury by Justice Hilbery and that if he had not fired the shot he should have only been convicted of manslaughter. The Court of Criminal Appeal dismissed the arguments of the two men saying that they were satisfied that Ostler had fired the fatal shot but with Appleby's encouragement so he was equally guilty. They were also satisfied that there was no misdirection by Justice Hilbery. The two men had been jointly involved in the break-in and were equally guilty of the murder of PC Shiell.

Appleby and Ostler were hanged on Thursday 11 July 1940 by Thomas Pierrepoint.

William Shiell's name is on the list of the national police force Roll of Honour in memory of those police officers of the United Kingdom who have lost their lives in the line of duty.

The Bloodstain, 1940

John Wright, who was forty-one, lived with his forty-three-year-old wife, Alice, and their three children at Pixley Hills, Toronto in Bishop Auckland. On 22 May, the three children came home from school for their lunch to find their mother lying unconscious on the kitchen floor. The children alerted the neighbours and medical help was called for.

Meanwhile, Wright came home and was told what had happened by a neighbour. He seemed very concerned and put his coat over his wife to keep her warm. When the doctors arrived Alice was found to have serious injuries consistent with having been violently beaten. She was taken to the Durham County Hospital where she died later that day.

The police conducted a search of the house and found a meat cleaver that looked to have traces of blood on the blade. When Wright was asked about the cleaver he said he had been using it the night before to chop firewood. Blood was also found on Wright's shirt. His explanation was that he had put the coat over his wife and when he had donned the coat again blood from it must have rubbed off onto his shirt. This would have been plausible except that he had also been wearing a waistcoat which would have protected his shirt from bloodstains when he put the coat back on. It was also discovered that, on the day of the murder, Wright had gone to an insurance office to verify that a life policy on Alice was still in place.

The trial was held at Leeds Assizes before Justice Stable on Thursday 25 July with CP Scott and GR Hinchcliffe acting for the prosecution and W Sexton for the defence. Wright pleaded not guilty but the evidence of the blood on his shirt and his interest in the insurance policy was enough for the jury to convict him. He was hanged by Thomas Pierrepoint on Tuesday 10 September.

No Recollection, 1940

Edward Scoller, aged forty-two, and his wife, Beatrice Barbara, who was thirty-five, lived at St Paul's Road in Middlesbrough. They had been married for a number of years when things began to turn sour. Between 1939 and 1940 the couple were having serious arguments and Beatrice left her husband more than once but always returned after a short period of time. On Wednesday 31 July 1940, Beatrice left again, perhaps meaning to stay away on this occasion.

Scoller's version of the events that followed were that on the afternoon of Monday 12 August he went on a drinking binge and then to work. He found he was incapable of working so left to go home. On the way he stopped for another couple of drinks and then decided he would find his wife and ask her to come home with him.

When Scoller found Beatrice she was with two friends, Mrs Hethage and Mrs Bunney. Beatrice walked off with her husband but told him she would not return to him unless they could get another house. He said the next thing he knew Beatrice was leaning on him with her arms around his neck. She fell to the ground and he thought she had fainted. He could not carry her so left her where she was lying and went home to get help.

Beatrice had been stabbed and was left on the ground to die. The police went to St Paul's Road to arrest Scoller and found he had tried to kill himself. He had first slashed his wrists and then tried to hang himself. Scoller was cut down and taken to hospital. Although the rope had cut deeply into his neck he survived and after five weeks in hospital was declared fit enough to stand trial.

His trial was held at York Assizes on 6 November before Justice Cassels with A Morley and Miles Archibald for the prosecution and GB Sykes for the defence. Scoller claimed he could not remember stabbing his wife. The jury decided that although he was drunk, he was carrying a knife and had then tried to commit suicide so was aware of his actions. Scoller was found guilty and hanged on Tuesday 24 December 1940 by Thomas Pierrepoint.

CHAPTER 28

An Unfaithful Paramour
1941

enry Lyndo White, who was thirty-nine, had lived with his wife, Annie, in Morton Street, South Shields but by 1941 the couple had been separated for some length of time. While still living with his wife the unemployed man had been having an affair which had being going on for about seven years. The 'other' woman was thirty-four-year-old Emily Wardle, a single lady that he had known for about thirteen years. Emily eventually told White she was finished with him as she had met someone else. White, although he was married with four children and had been unfaithful, could not stand the thought of the same thing being done to him.

At about 6.20 pm on Sunday 19 January an apprentice joiner, William Elliott, was going home from work along Bertram Street when he saw White with Emily. White had her pinned against a wall and was hitting her in the face. Elliott told the man to leave her alone but White refused. Elliott walked away but worried about the situation, he turned around. As he did so he saw White put his hand in his pocket and, taking out a razor, slashed at Emily with the weapon. She fell to the ground with terrible wounds to her throat. Elliott ran back to assist and helped her into a nearby shop at 47 Bertram Street. White stood on the other side of the road watching the proceedings. Elliott went for the police leaving Emily with the shopkeeper, Ernest Unwin. White then walked into the shop and, as Emily lay dying, said: 'I told you I would kill you, meeting someone else and double crossing me.' When she died a few minutes later White said to Unwin: 'If there is one there is going to be two.' He then slashed his own throat and wrists with the razor.

White was treated in hospital and lived to stand trial for Emily's murder at Durham Assizes before Justice Charles on

South Shields where Henry White murdered Emily Wardle in 1941.
Author's collection

Friday 14 February, with J Charlesworth acting for the prosecution and JH Robson for the defence. On Elliott's and Unwin's testimony White was found guilty of wilful murder. Annie White was in court and fainted when she heard the verdict. White was hanged on Thursday 6 March 1941 by Thomas Pierrepoint.

Murder of a Blind Man, 1941

At 10.30 on the morning of Wednesday 11 June, William Anderson, a sixty-three-year-old blind man was found at his home with severe head injuries. He lived at 9 Moor End Terrace, Belmont near Durham with his nephew, Joseph Robert Anderson. The injured man was taken by ambulance to the Durham County Hospital. The police found an axe in the house which had evidently been the weapon used to attack the blind man. The house had been ransacked so the motive appeared to be robbery.

That morning, Joseph, who was a postman, had left for work at his usual time of just after 7 am. He gave his uncle breakfast and then left knowing that the housekeeper, Ethel Carr, would arrive at about 10 am. When Ethel arrived the door was locked so after knocking for a time and receiving no answer she went to number 8 of the same street to see if William's brother, Alfred, had a key. He did not but seeing that an upstairs window was open he procured a ladder and climbed up and into the house. William was lying near the front door, barely alive.

Enquiries by the police led them to set up a search for Edward Walker Anderson, great nephew of the injured man. Anderson was nineteen and the son of Joseph Anderson. He had been employed at the *Grand Hotel* in Tynemouth as a porter but had left in March. On 7 June, he had returned to the hotel and had been given accommodation for the night. The following morning the manageress had taken pity on Anderson and had given him £1 because he had no money.

The police went to Anderson's home at 52 Tadman Street in Hull and searched the premises where they found articles that had been stolen from Bertram Street. Edward Anderson admitted to assault and robbery as soon as he was arrested. When his great uncle died from his injuries on Thursday 19 June the charge became one of murder.

He was committed to stand trial at Leeds Assizes on Friday 11 July before Justice Croom-Johnson with A Morley for the prosecution and JS Snowden for the defence.

Anderson pleaded not guilty to murder saying that his victim was still alive when he left the scene. The defence stated that Anderson had been very short of money and on 11 June he had waited until his father had left the Moor End Terrace house to go to work. Anderson had gone to the shed, found an axe and had then entered the house and attacked William. While his great uncle was lying on the floor unconscious and bleeding Anderson ransacked the house stealing money and other items. He then took a bus to Darlington and from there went to Hull. There was a query from the defence on whether the injuries that Anderson had inflicted had caused William's death or something could have happened between him being taken in the ambulance and seeing a doctor at the hospital. The judge agreed that this was a matter for concern and adjourned the case while this defect in the evidence was looked into as it had to be proved beyond a doubt that Anderson was the murderer.

Medical evidence established that death had been directly caused by the horrific injuries inflicted with the axe. The case resumed the following morning and, after the summing up of all the evidence, the jury of nine men and three women found Anderson guilty of wilful murder. He was sentenced to death and hanged on Thursday 31 July 1941 by Thomas Pierrepoint.

CHAPTER 29

The Rape of a Newly-wed 1942

argaret Mary was a WAAF Corporal from Wintry Park, Epping in Essex and had been billeted at Kenton since September of 1941. She and Second Lieutenant Patrick Leslie Rice of the Royal Artillery had been married on Tuesday 21 April 1942. Less than two months after their marriage, on Saturday 13 June, Margaret went to Newcastle Central railway station with her husband to see him off on the London train after he had been at home on a short leave. He intended catching the 12.40 am train but there was standing room only so they waited for the next train which left at 1.05 am.

After waving her husband off, whether it was because she could not get a taxi or by choice, Margaret set off to walk back to her billet in the early hours of the morning. She was twenty-four, very fit and athletic and would have thought nothing of making the three and a half mile journey on foot as she often walked from Newcastle.

An extract of a map showing the location of Park Terrace, Framlington Place and the location of Margaret Rice's murder. Ordnance Survey Central Newcastle 1914

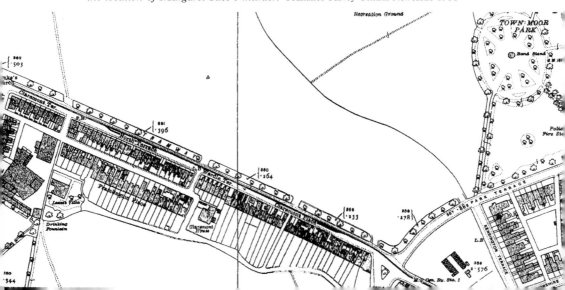

An early view of Newcastle Central Railway Station. Margaret Rice waved her husband off from here and was returning home when she was murdered.
Author's collection

At 8.30 on Saturday morning James Jones, a milkman, was delivering along Claremont Road, Town Moor when he saw Margaret's partially clothed body lying on the grass verge partially hidden behind a water pipe. It was immediately obvious that she had suffered a frenzied attack as she had numerous, jagged wounds to her head.

The police were called and a thorough search of the area was carried out. Beside the body pieces of vulcanite were found. This was a mineral sometimes used to make gun handles. A post-mortem revealed that Margaret had been raped and a blunt object had been used to inflict her injuries. It was assumed, because of the broken gun handle, that this was the murder weapon. She had also been robbed as, amongst other articles, her wedding and engagement rings were missing. It was believed by the police that because of the violent frenzy in which the attack had been carried out that the motive had been sexual and the robbery was probably an afterthought. On notifying Margaret's husband of the tragedy he immediately returned from the South.

When the police began their appeal for anyone with information William Ambrose Collins, a twenty-one-year-old merchant navy ship's apprentice, came forward and told the police that he had been in the area around the time the attack took place. He told the police that he did not want to become a suspect so thought he would tell them of his movements voluntarily.

Collins' story was that he had met up with a friend, Edward Bircham Morgan, at the *Royal Oak* pub on the Friday evening. They were at Newcastle Station at 12.30 am on Saturday having a coffee. Morgan had then dropped Collins off at Park Terrace which was near to his home at 17 Framlington Place. The police paid a visit to Morgan who corroborated Collins' story but he also added that he had sold Collins a revolver on the Friday night. The police went to Collins' house and conducted a search. They found a revolver with a broken vulcanite handle under a bolster and a piece of the handle in a suitcase. The pieces of vulcanite found at the scene of the crime and the piece in the suitcase matched up to make the broken handle of the weapon complete proving that it was the gun that was used to commit the crime.

Collins' trial began at Northumberland Assizes before Justice Cassels on Wednesday 26 August with CP Scott and J Charlesworth acting for the prosecution and JH Robson for the defence. The defence tried to plead temporary insanity, stating that Collins had sustained a head injury four years previously and it had affected him so he was not responsible for his actions, especially when he was under the influence of alcohol.

Dr BG Derry, the medical officer at Durham Gaol, told the court that he had found the prisoner to be of sound mind but that alcohol could produce a state of mind which may lead to acts of extreme violence. The trial lasted two days with the end result being a verdict of guilty and the death sentence being passed. Collins was hanged on Wednesday 28 October 1942 by Thomas Pierrepoint.

Margaret Rice, the newlywed who was murdered by William Collins in 1949. Author's collection

CHAPTER 30

Murder of a Flight Sergeant 1944

Sydney James Delasalle was thirty-nine and an aircraftman in the RAF at Chingford, Essex. The Flight Sergeant of his regiment was Ronald John Murphy who was twenty-three and came from Lowther Road in Brighton. In February 1944, some of the regiment were stationed at a camp in the North of England.

On the morning of Wednesday 2 February, Murphy and Corporal Archibald Taylor were inspecting beds. In a later statement given by Taylor, when they arrived at Delasalle's hut, he had said to Murphy that he wanted an argument with him about the rations. Murphy reminded Delasalle that he outranked him and told him that the rations had been taken to the men's cookhouse and that they were none of his business anyway. He then added that if there was any more insolence he would be instructed to appear before the station commander. Delasalle then apparently challenged Murphy to a fight by saying: 'I would like to see you outside with your coat off.' Murphy put a charge on Delasalle for insubordination and, two days later, on 4 February, he appeared before the station commander. Delasalle told him that it was Murphy who had told him 'he would see him in the morning' but the commander would have nothing said against the NCOs and would not even consider any suggestion that they had been lying. Delasalle was ordered to be confined to barracks for fourteen days as punishment for his insubordination.

A little later that day the NAAFI van drew up and the men, including Murphy, began to queue for tea. Delasalle was seen walking toward the line of men carrying a rifle. He shouted to them to stand clear, put the rifle to his shoulder and fired a shot. He then reloaded and fired a second shot. Both shots

An army camp in the North of England such as the one where Sydney James Delasalle shot and killed Ronald John Murphy in 1944. Author's collection

hit Murphy, the second in the heart which caused instant death. Four other men in the queue were also injured but all recovered.

Delasalle was immediately arrested and charged with murder. He stood trial at Leeds Assizes on Wednesday 22 March before Justice Hallett with CP Scott and Ralph Cleworth for the prosecution and G Streatfield and William Temple for the defence.

At the trial Delasalle stated that he was unable to say what had happened because, after the incident about the rations, his mind was a blank and he remembered nothing until after the shooting when he found himself lying on the ground and held down by some of the men from his regiment. Witnesses came forward to testify that, prior to the shooting, Delasalle had been a quiet, inoffensive man who had never been in trouble. He was described as being a good worker and well liked. One witness statement differed from the rest, that of LAC Herbert Rigg. He said that he was quite certain that after the shots had been fired he had heard Delasalle mumble: 'He asked for it.'

Delasalle's defence put forward a plea of guilty but with temporary insanity. Medical opinion was given on loss of memory and Dr Macadam suggested that Delasalle might not have been aware of his movements at the time the crime was committed. The plea was not accepted and the jury found him guilty of wilful murder and he was sentenced to death. He was hanged by Albert Pierrepoint on Thursday 13 April 1944.

CHAPTER 31

The Jealous Marine
1946

Sarah Jean Young, known as Jean, was nineteen and lived with her parents, a brother, George, and two sisters, Edith and Isabelle, at Crummock Bank Farm, Waverton. Her father, also named George, had worked the farm for fourteen years. The Youngs were known as charitable people always ready to help in a good cause. Jean was described as a likable girl who enjoyed going to dances and other events when her day's work on the farm was finished.

At about 8.40 on the evening of Monday 19 November 1945, Mr and Mrs Young were in an adjoining room and their children were sitting round the fire in the kitchen as they often did on a cold winter's evening. The Youngs could not have known that this particular evening was to be very different. The siblings were looking through some old photographs when, suddenly, there was a loud crack and the sound of breaking glass. Before anyone realised that the noise was a shot that had been fired through the kitchen window, Jean slumped forward into the fire. Her family moved her away from the fire but she was unconscious. Mr Young drove his car to the nearest telephone to summon a doctor and the police. Although Dr T Dolan and Dr Rankine arrived very quickly it was too late to help Jean, the injury from the bullet had proven fatal.

At 9.45 that same evening a marine, carrying a rifle, walked into the Reading Room in Waverton. He told a group of young men that were playing snooker that he had shot someone and they should telephone for the police. The man was Charles Edward Prescott who was twenty-three and a Royal Marine. He lived with his parents and his brother, also a soldier, at Biglands in Wigton.

When the police arrived Prescott was holding the rifle from which he ejected a cartridge. Another twenty-four rounds of ammunition were found in his pockets. He was taken into custody and charged with feloniously, wilfully and with malice aforethought of the murder of Jean Young.

Prescott had been courting eighteen-year-old Isabelle Young, better known as Belle, but he had been insanely jealous. After seeing her at a dance with another man on the night of Wednesday 17 October he had threatened to shoot her. Her feelings for Prescott had already waned so after this occurrence she finished the relationship but told him she would like them to remain friends. Four days later Prescott threatened Belle with a dagger but she managed to take it from him and throw it away. Perhaps if the threats had been taken more seriously and reported to the police the tragedy may have been averted.

Prescott's trial was held on Tuesday 15 January 1946 before Justice Lynskey at Durham Assizes with W Gorman and S Lloyd acting for the prosecution and Denis Gerrard and RS Nicklin for the defence. The defence put forward a plea of accidental death saying that Prescott had only gone to the farm to see Belle and had left his rifle leaning on a fence while he walked up and down trying to attract her attention. He had heard a noise and being startled had knocked the rifle which had gone off accidentally. Five witnesses testified that when Prescott had gone into the Reading Room after the shooting he had commented that he hoped he had shot the right person as there were a lot of people in the kitchen and he had fired from some distance away. Prescott had also told an officer that on 7 November he had been hiding behind a hedge waiting 'to do his girl in'.

The members of the jury all agreed that Prescott's story was a tissue of lies and the shooting was intended except that he had killed the wrong girl. They brought in a unanimous verdict of guilty and he received sentence of death. The appeal for a reprieve was denied by the Home Secretary and Prescott was hanged on Tuesday 5 March 1946 by Thomas Pierrepoint.

Shipmates, 1946

Arthur Charles was a thirty-four-year-old African seaman. He had moved in with Hannah Burns at 14 Albermarle Street in South Shields. Hannah was married but separated from her husband. In November 1944, while Charles was at sea, Hannah took up with another seaman, John Duplessis. At the end of November Charles returned to find Duplessis in Hannah's house. An argument took place and the police were called. PC Welsh attended and Duplessis was escorted from the premises. Eventually Hannah and Charles drifted apart and, in the middle of 1945, he moved out of the house and into lodgings at Dean Street.

In September of that year Duplessis and Charles took work on the same ship. The stint finished on 28 November and both men travelled back to South Shields. On Thursday 29 November Hannah and Duplessis were together at the *Locomotive Inn*. Charles was also there having a drink. Later, Hannah and Duplessis went back to her house. Duplessis went to bed and Hannah stayed up to tidy around. She went to the back door and was shocked to see Charles standing there holding a revolver. He pushed past her and going to the man he saw as his rival, challenged him to a fight. Duplessis refused but Charles persisted until eventually the former said: 'Shoot if you're going to shoot.' Charles answered saying: 'I have been waiting for this.' With those words he fired six bullets, five of which hit his victim. Hannah had run out to alert the police and Charles was later arrested at his lodgings and charged with the shooting. Septicaemia from the wounds spread through his body and Duplessis died five weeks later on Monday 31 December. The charge against Charles was then one of murder.

The trial was held on Thursday 14 February 1946, before Justice Oliver at Durham Assizes with J Charlesworth for the prosecution and W Temple for the defence. Charles pleaded not guilty and stated that he had been nowhere near Hannah's house that night and had never possessed a revolver. Duplessis had signed a deposition before he died naming Charles as his attacker.

There was also Hannah's testimony. A few weeks before the trial began a child playing near the railway had found a revolver that held six empty cartridge cases. Hannah identified the weapon as the one she had seen in Charles' hand. The jury brought in a verdict of guilty and after an unsuccessful appeal Charles was hanged on Tuesday 26 March 1946 by Steve Wade.

CHAPTER 32

The Body in the Field
1949

On Sunday 14 August 1949, there was a report to the police of a murder having taken place in a cornfield at Cold Hesledon. Detective Inspector Rowell went to the field at 6.40 am and found the body of a woman. He later stated that she looked as though she had been attacked by a wild animal. She had been beaten, her clothing torn and after being raped she had been strangled with her own scarf. The woman was Mrs Lily Nightingale who was twenty-nine and the mother of two children, John aged six and Daniel aged four. Her husband, Thomas, was a seaman in the Merchant Navy and had left his family on 9 August to rejoin his ship. When her husband was away Lily stayed with her father, James Hodgson,

The village of Easington Colliery where Lily Nightingale had been living with her father at the time of her brutal rape and murder in 1949. Author's collection

at 5 Bolam Street in Easington Colliery to act as housekeeper for him.

In the early hours of Sunday morning John Wilson, a twenty-six-year-old miner who lived at Alfred Street in Murton, had gone to his sister's house and told her he had murdered a woman but she did not believe him. He then went to his father's house where he eventually convinced him and his brother that he really had killed someone and so they had called the police. Rowell arrested Wilson at 7.30 am at his father's house and from there he was taken to Houghton-le-Spring police station where he was charged with the murder. The police found it easy to trace Lily's movements prior to her death as she had been seen by numerous witnesses. It was quickly established that she had met a man at the *King's Head* in Easington on Friday night. The man was identified as Wilson. Further information determined that the couple had met up the following day and had gone from pub to pub talking to and being seen by a number of acquaintances. On Saturday night they were spotted walking across the fields towards the place where Lily's body was found.

After an initial sitting before Seaham magistrates he was committed to stand trial at Durham Assizes on 2 November before Justice Oliver, with CB Fenwick and C Cohen for the prosecution and FBH Hylton-Foster for his defence. Wilson's reason for the murder was that when he suggested he and Lily make love she had asked for money which caused him to fly into a rage and attack and rape her. The defence suggested that, although there was no doubt that Wilson was the perpetrator, because he had drink in him he would have been more likely to have been provoked than if he had been sober so the charge should be manslaughter. The jury did not agree because of the callous, revolting manner of the attack and returned a verdict of guilty of wilful murder which brought with it the sentence of death.

John Wilson was hanged on 13 December 1949 in a double execution with Benjamin Roberts. Four executioners were employed on this occasion. Steve Wade was assisted by Syd Dernley, Harry Allen and Harry Kirk. This was to be Dernley's and Allen's first execution.

Unrequited Love, 1949

On Sunday 14 August 1949, while the police were still questioning John Wilson about his attack on Lily Nightingale, another murder took place not too far away, that of a twenty-one-year-old girl, Lillian Vickers. Lillian lived in Burns Road, Chilton Buildings and was employed as a laundry worker. She was described as an attractive, happy girl who was looking forward to a holiday in Blackpool that she had booked a few weeks earlier.

On Sunday evening Lillian had been to the cinema at Darlington, which was about fifteen miles away, returning on the last bus of the night. When she stepped off the bus she was met by Benjamin Roberts and Alan Neal. Roberts, who was a miner, was twenty-three and lived opposite Lillian in Raby Terrace. All three friends went into Roberts' home for a while with Lillian and Neal leaving at just after 11 pm. At about 11.30 pm Mrs Vickers looked out of the window and had seen her daughter and Neal talking at her front gate. While the couple were indulging in a kiss Roberts came across the road in his shirt sleeves. Wanting some privacy, Neal led Lillian around to the back of the houses where there was a shed near a fence which enclosed some allotments.

Mrs Vickers, meanwhile, had gone to bed and was just dozing off when she heard a shot. At first she assumed it was someone shooting at rats, which had been seen in the neighbourhood recently but seconds later she heard another shot. Realizing that her daughter was not in the house she got dressed and went outside to be greeted by a neighbour telling her that Lillian had been injured. Neal and Lillian had been behind the shed when Roberts approached them carrying a gun which was pointed in their direction. Neal asked him what he thought he was doing and Roberts replied that the gun was loaded. Lillian walked towards Roberts saying to him: 'Benny, don't be so soft.' At that moment the gun went off and Lillian dropped to the ground. As Neal ran off in terror he heard another shot. Going towards the village he bumped into Roberts' father who was coming to investigate. Neal led him to the back of the shed where Lillian had fallen. She was dead and Roberts was lying face down across her body still alive after having shot himself. His father's double barrelled-sporting gun was on the ground beside him. By the time the doctor and the police had arrived Roberts had disappeared. He was eventually found some distance from Lillian's body evidently having crawled away. Under police guard, Roberts was taken to Newcastle General Hospital where he was treated for the gunshot wound to his head which had also caused an injury to his neck.

The police soon pieced together the whole scenario which had obviously been a crime of passion with a motive of jealousy. Roberts had known Lillian since childhood and was totally infatuated with her but she looked on him only as a friend. The week before the shooting he had spoken to Mrs Vickers, telling her of his feelings. Knowing she had preferred Neal in the romantic stakes, Roberts had become insanely jealous and when he saw his friend kissing the girl of his dreams something had snapped and he had decided if he could not have her then no one would. Neal stated that he and Roberts had been friends for some time. When he and Lillian had become attracted to each other there had been nothing to suggest that Roberts had resented the relationship in any way.

Roberts had recovered sufficiently from his injury to stand trial at Durham Assizes on Monday 31 October before Justice Oliver with CB Fenwick and Norman S Harper for the prosecution and Ralph Cleworth and W Temple acting in his defence. His plea was that the shooting had been accidental. When he realised he had shot Lillian he had turned the gun on himself. The jury did not believe this version and that the truth was that the shooting had been intentional. After a verdict of guilty was brought sentence of death was passed.

The executions of John Wilson and Benjamin Roberts were provisionally fixed for 22 November but were postponed pending appeals to the Criminal Court of Appeal. Both appeals were denied and the double execution was re-scheduled for Tuesday 13 December 1949.

When a person who was to be executed had a throat wound, usually from a suicide attempt, it meant that the hangman had to perform his task with extra precision. If the injury had not completely healed there was a risk that the noose, if not placed correctly, could open the wound. This, at best, could offer a gruesome spectacle and, at worst, could mean decapitation. The authorities needed it to be seen that justice was carried out in a humane manner. Steve Wade, as principal executioner at the double execution, had this added problem concerning Roberts who had sustained just such a neck injury so the preparations the evening before the executions were carried out with extra care. The apparatus was meticulously tested using sand bags to ensure the smooth operation so that as the lever was pulled both men would drop to their deaths simultaneously and instantly.

A double execution, from start to finish, should only have taken about fifteen seconds but all the extra care of the previous evening did not allow for the events of that morning. The wing was eerily silent as the four executioners made their way to the condemned cells to pinion the prisoners' arms and then escort them to the scaffold. They were almost at their destination when the silence was suddenly shattered by the sound of singing which came from the cell Roberts was occupying. In a trembling voice he was singing a hymn with the much stronger voice of the priest as accompaniment. Kirk and Allen headed for that cell while Wade and Dernley went for Wilson. Within a few second Wilson was in place on the trap door, hood over his face and noose around his neck but there was no sign of Roberts. The officials and the executioners all looked towards the open door with pale worried faces while at least forty-five seconds ticked by. Wilson suddenly began to sway and seeing that the hooded man was about to pass out, one of the warders, with a look of absolute horror on his face, stepped forward to assist. If Wilson fell with the noose around his neck there was no telling what the outcome would have been but he would probably have been partially strangled before the noose could have been removed. Just at that moment the two executioners appeared with Roberts. In a split second they had him hooded and noosed and the trap lever was sprung. It was over, but those few extra seconds must have been like an eternity to Wilson and nearly caused a complete shambles. When Kirk and Allen had gone to get Roberts he wanted to carry on singing and had decided he was not going to the scaffold. The delay had been caused by Roberts refusing to lift his arms for the straps to be put in place and the executioners had to do it by force.

CHAPTER 33

Strangled
1950

George Finlay Brown, a twenty-three-year-old labourer, had been living at 26 King Street in North Shields with Mrs Mary Victoria Longhurst who was the same age. After living together for about six weeks Brown moved into 52 Princes Street. Although they did not reside in the same house any longer the pair still kept company but Mary was also seeing another man, Frank Dougal Bouchier, and had told Brown that she might go to live with him. This revelation must have upset Brown as he was seen arguing with Mary in the street on Thursday 9 March 1950. They must, for a short time at least, have settled their differences as Brown slept at Mary's house that same night. The following day trouble flared up again and Mary went to the police and put in a complaint against Brown. This resulted in the police giving Brown a warning and telling him to stay away from her.

On Friday 10 March, at just before 11 pm, a neighbour heard thudding footsteps and then shouting and screaming coming from Mary's rooms. He became worried and contacted the police. When the police arrived it was to find Mary's body lying on her bed with her young daughter, in a state of sheer terror, beside her. Mary had been strangled with a cord which had then been attached to the foot of her bed holding her head in a murderous grip.

Brown was immediately arrested and charged with murder. On Tuesday 30 May he stood trial at Newcastle Assizes before Justice Morris with EG Robey and F Hylton-Foster for the prosecution and H Shepherd for the defence. Brown denied all knowledge of the crime. He said he had been to a pub for a drink and had then gone for a walk. There was nothing and no

Newcastle Assizes where the trial of George Brown was held in 1950. The author

one to substantiate his alibi and the jury took just thirty minutes
to find him guilty of Mary's murder. George Brown was hanged
on Tuesday 11 July 1950 by Albert Pierrepoint.

A Strange Arrangement, 1950

Francis Henry Wilson was known to be violent towards his wife,
Gladys. The couple had lived in Shildon in, by all accounts, a
rather unhappy marriage. In 1944, they had met John Walker,
who at that time was in the army. Perhaps not surprisingly an
affair began between Walker and Gladys. The Wilsons moved
to Station Road in Brompton and when Walker was demobbed
in 1947 he moved in as their lodger. Before long, in a rather
bizarre arrangement, Gladys was sleeping with Walker while her
husband had the small back bedroom. The violence towards
Gladys had all but ceased with Walker there as her protector.

Gladys always handled the money and gave her husband 10s
(50p) a week for himself. On Saturday 29 April 1950, for some
reason that never came to light, she gave Wilson just 5s (25p)
which did not please him at all. Gladys went off to the pictures
that evening leaving Wilson and Walker together in the house.
When she returned home at about 11 pm there was no sign of

York Assizes where the trial of John Walker was held in 1950. Author's collection

her husband. Gladys was not concerned as she assumed he had gone to bed early. The following morning, Walker woke Gladys and, after giving her a cup of tea, told her he was leaving as he had killed her husband. He said that when she had left the house the previous evening Wilson had started complaining about being short changed with his pocket money. He had told Walker that when he got Gladys on her own he was going to beat her. After his confession Walker then left the house on his bicycle leaving Gladys to deal with the aftermath of his actions. Wilson's body was in the scullery at the back of the kitchen. He had been struck six times with an axe that still lay on the floor beside him.

Walker was picked up by the police at Bishop Auckland later that day. He stood trial on Thursday 22 June at York Assizes before Justice Croom-Johnson with H Shepherd and John M McLuskey acting for the prosecution and H Robson for the defence. He maintained a defence that he had killed Wilson to protect Gladys from violence. It was not a defence that gained him any sympathy from the jury, especially with the violent manner of the murderous attack, and he was found guilty. Walker was hanged on Thursday 13 July 1950 by Steve Wade.

The Man who Wanted to Hang, 1950
On Saturday 22 July 1950, an old cargo ship made her way up the River Tees to dock at Billingham Reach Wharf. She was the SS *Absalom* which had been built in 1898 at William Gray's

yard in West Hartlepool. She would be in port for a few days while her cargo of sugar was unloaded. The third engineer on the ship was Patrick George Turnage who had been born in India. He was thirty-one and his home was near Durban in South Africa.

When ships docked at port, after long periods at sea, it was commonplace for many of the crew to go ashore and let off steam by spending their wages on drink and women. Turnage was given the Saturday night off so he took an early bus into the town to look for alcohol and female company. On asking the bus conductor where he might find these two commodities he was directed to the *Victoria Hotel* in Joseph Street.

Seventy-eight-year-old Julia Beesley had been widowed twenty-five years earlier and now lived with her son, Robert, at Northbourne Road in Stockton. For the most part Julia employed herself as an active member of an old person's club but she still plied her trade as a prostitute. At weekends, Julia would dress up and go around the pubs looking for customers. Understandably, with her not being in the prime of her life, she would suffer many a rejection. The night of Saturday 29 October was no exception. Julia went from pub to pub but did not manage to entice a client. She arrived at the *Victoria Hotel* in the late evening. By this time, having had a drink or two in every pub she had visited, she could hardly stand but still managed to carry on drinking and talking to the men at the bar. Tom Davies, who was the holiday relief manager, watched her in case she became a nuisance to his customers. He eventually lost sight of Julia and assumed she had left but he was mistaken. She had gone into the buffet bar where Turnage was drinking who was also very drunk by this time. Julia latched onto him and after the two went for some supper together Turnage asked her to come back to his ship for a drink. She agreed and Turnage flagged a taxi down. When they arrived at the ship's moorings Julia asked if the taxi was going to wait for her. Turnage told her he would tell the driver to return later but as he paid the fare he whispered to the driver that she was going to stay all night. What Turnage did not know was that Julia never spent all night with a client and sending the taxi away upset her. The watchman on the *Absalom* saw the taxi leave and then heard the couple arguing. Julia walked away and after a few minutes Turnage followed her. When Turnage arrived back at the ship an hour or so later the watchman asked if he had found the woman and he said he had not. The following morning, when Julia had not returned home, her son called the police.

All was a flurry of activity on the *Absalom* as preparations were being made for her to sail on the early evening tide. If the ship had sailed before Julia's body was found Turnage would probably never have been caught. He would have, in all probability, left the ship at the next port and disappeared. He was not to be so lucky. John Walker, a navvy, was cycling home for his Sunday dinner when something in the ditch at the side of the lane caught his eye. On entering the ditch and pulling aside some grass he was horrified to see the body of a woman and he immediately alerted the police. They were baffled as to how Julia had met her death because no marks were visible on the body. A post-mortem carried out by a Home Office pathologist, Dr David Price, revealed that she had been strangled. The examiner said that it had taken very little pressure to kill Julia and it had been caused by her clothing tightening around her neck.

It now appeared that this was possibly a murder and it was not difficult for the police to follow Julia's movements of the previous evening and at 5.30 pm, just before the ship was to sail, Turnage was arrested. His initial story was that Julia had made sexual suggestions to him. He had told her she was too old, old enough to be his mother, and then he had pushed her and she fell. Julia's death had not been caused by a fall but it would be difficult to prove she was murdered as it could have just as easily been a tragic accident. The angle at which she fell could have caused her clothes to pull and tighten around her neck causing her to strangle. The interrogators questioning Turnage knew that his explanation of refusing sexual advances was not true as it had been established that he had been looking for a prostitute. The taxi driver had been told that Julia was staying the night so Turnage obviously intended to take her aboard the ship and sleep with her and the watchman had heard part of the argument. The detectives on the case wanted Turnage to be charged with murder but knew that he would almost certainly get away with manslaughter. The jury would be unsympathetic to a prostitute of Julia's age and background. There was also the fact that it had taken very little violence to kill her.

After much initial preparation the trial was set for Saturday 28 October at Durham Assizes before Justice Hallett. Two days before the trial was to begin Turnage asked to see Detective Chief Inspector John Rowell. The detective was flabbergasted when Turnage told him he was going to plead guilty to murder. His lead defence solicitor, Herbert Shepherd, was summoned but Turnage would not change his mind. He was told that if he pleaded guilty to the capital charge of murder there would be no jury and he was putting the noose around his own neck. Turnage signed a statement saying he was guilty to premeditated murder. He said the old tart had asked him for £1 for her services so he had killed her. The reason Turnage gave for admitting to the murder was he found the prospect of hanging preferable to spending fifteen years in prison. His trial was brought forward to Thursday 26 October with Police Inspector Rowell the only witness called. The entire proceedings only lasted seven minutes, just long enough for sentence of death to be passed by Justice Hallett.

Steve Wade, assisted by Syd Dernley, hanged Turnage on Tuesday 14 November 1950. Dernley's later comment was, that as the cell door was opened for Turnage to be taken to the gallows, the seaman turned and looked at his escorts. For a moment there was a flicker of fear and then, in a spine chilling way, he smiled. The prison wardens and other officials who attended Turnage before and during his walk to the gallows said that he was cheerful and was looking forward to the end. It was quite common for a kind of sympathetic friendship to form between a warder and a condemned prisoner as they would spend days, sometimes weeks, in close proximity in a tiny cell. The warder would play cards, talk and sooth when the strain became too much. Because of the close involvement these warders were removed from the cell an hour or two before the execution and strangers brought in for the final preparations. In the case of Turnage, a request that the warder that had been his soul mate could stay with him until he breathed his last was

156 of the twentieth century

granted. All that were involved in this case felt that the situation was bizarre as not one of them would have chosen death over life. Perhaps Turnage was weighed down by guilt of what he had done and knew long years in prison would have given him too much time to dwell on his crime. Then again he was a seaman who was used to wide open spaces and perhaps he really just could not face the thought of years of confinement in a tiny cell.

CHAPTER 34

The Seamen
1952

Evelyn McDonald, who was twenty-five, lived with Montez Ullah, a Bengali seaman. About five years into the relationship, when Ullah was away at sea, Evelyn moved in with thirty-nine-year-old Tahir Ali. Ali was Ullah's cousin and was also a seaman. Evelyn must have been rather fickle because when Ali returned from a voyage she was back with Ullah. The couple were living in Adelaide Street in South Shields along with a friend of Evelyn's, Mary Lucas. In November, there was a fierce argument between Ali and Evelyn with Mary having to separate the pair. Ali then threatened both women saying he would finish Evelyn and if Mary interfered he would finish her too. The situation then seemed to calm itself.

On the evening of 20 November 1951, Evelyn, Mary, Ali and Evelyn's mother went out for a drink together. Evelyn's mother left the pub at about 10 pm and the other three left together a little later. Ali asked Evelyn to go home with him but she refused and they started fighting. During the struggle Ali pulled out a flick knife and stabbed Evelyn twice in the back and once in the chest. The wounds punctured Evelyn's lungs and severed the pulmonary artery.

When he was arrested Ali seemed unperturbed by his actions. He told the police that he had spent hundreds of pounds on Evelyn and she had used him and taken him for a fool.

His trial was heard at Durham Assizes before Justice Hallett on 31 January 1952 with Herbert Shepherd and Gordon Smith acting for the prosecution and GS Waller and W Johnson for the defence. When Ali was found guilty of murder and sentenced to death a plea for mercy by the Moslem population was passed to the Prime Minister of Pakistan but to no avail. Ali was hanged on Friday 21 March 1952.

The Wedding Party, 1952
Herbert Appleby lived at Laing Street, Grangetown near Middlesbrough. He was twenty and was employed in the steelworks as a sling-loader. On the evening of Saturday 20 September 1952, a celebration that Appleby attended turned into a nightmare for him and everybody concerned. Appleby was later described as a quiet, well-mannered youth with his actions that evening being totally out of character.

John David Thomas was twenty-nine and worked as a shipyard fitter. He lived at 18 Lee Road in Grangetown. Thomas's stepbrother had been married and afterwards there was a party at Thomas's house to which Appleby and his girlfriend, Lillian Robbins, better known as Dolly, were invited. Appleby had eaten little food and had not slept much in the hours previous but consumed a large amount of alcohol at the celebrations. He had walked into the sitting room to see Thomas and Dolly side by side on the settee. He said afterwards that Thomas had his arm around Dolly's waist and he thought that there was something going on between them.

Appleby walked to his own home, which was nearby, picked up a carving knife, and returning to the party, plunged it into Thomas's chest. Thomas died within minutes of being stabbed. Appleby left the house and took a taxi to the police station and told Sergeant Ellis that he had stabbed and killed a man. Appleby was arrested and while awaiting trial was examined by Dr TM Cuthbert of St Luke's Mental Hospital in Middlesbrough. He was also examined by Dr IGW Pickering, a medical officer at Durham Gaol.

Abbleby stood trial on Thursday 4 December 1952 at Leeds Assizes before Justice Cassels with Herbert Shepherd and J McLuskey for the prosecution and G Hinchcliffe and TR Nevin for the defence. His plea was not guilty on the grounds of insanity. His father, Frederick, testified that his son had tried to commit suicide in April of 1950 by putting his head in a gas oven but had no recollection of doing so on the following day.

Medical opinion from Dr Cuthbert was that Appleby was insane through alcohol at the time of the murder. Also that he had inherited a temperamental form of instability. Dr Pickering's evidence was conflicting. He stated that in his opinion Appleby was not suffering from any certifiable disease of the mind. His jealousy would have given him powerful emotions but that was not to say that he did not know that what he was doing was wrong.

Dolly, of Pearl Street, Middlesbrough, stated that she was to become engaged to Appleby on 19 October which was her birthday. He had once said to her, she had thought jokingly, that if she went out with another man Appleby would kill him. Dolly added that what Appleby had seen between her and Thomas could probably be described as a mild flirtation. When Appleby had entered the room with the knife he had a blank expression on his face, as if he was miles away. Dolly said she had jumped up from the settee but did not see what happened next as she had turned her head away.

At the end of the trial, which lasted two days, the jury found Appleby guilty of wilful murder. An appeal petition was signed with more than 12,000 signatures and sent, along with the medical evidence, to the Home Secretary. The appeal was denied and Appleby was hanged at Durham on Wednesday 24 December 1952. A notice was pinned to the door of the gaol signed by Dr Pickering, Rev Bertram Wilson and the prison governor, John Richards, stating that justice had been served.

CHAPTER 35

The Carlisle Shopkeeper 1957

ohn Willson Vickers was twenty-two when he decided to rob a small sweet and grocery shop at 36 Tait Street, Carlisle. He probably thought that he could be in and out without discovery as the owner of the shop was a seventy-two-year-old lady and slightly deaf. Vickers was mistaken in thinking that Jane Duckett was an easy target as things went horribly wrong when she was disturbed by a noise he had made on entering the building. Jane came down the stairs in her nightclothes and confronted the intruder in an attempt to protect her property. Vickers hit the elderly lady a number of times before searching the premises and then fleeing, leaving his victim where she had fallen.

On Sunday 14 April, ten-year-old Michael Butcher noticed the blinds to Jane's shop were still closed and her milk was still on the doorstep just before lunchtime. He told his parents and, knowing the old lady was usually an early riser, Mr Butcher went to investigate and looking through a broken window he saw Jane lying at the bottom of the stairs. He alerted a police woman who was nearby and she summoned Detective Inspector Blair and an ambulance. When the officials had forced their way into the property it was to find the elderly lady already dead. A local police surgeon suspected that there had been foul play so a huge police hunt for the perpetrator was set in motion. Posters were put up, door to door enquiries made, cars and lorries stopped and their drivers were questioned. Meanwhile a post-mortem had been carried out on the body by a pathologist who confirmed that Jane had been beaten and at her age the shock caused by the moderately severe injuries were enough to cause death.

THE

Carlisle Journal

With which is Incorporated the "Carlisle Express and Examiner" and the "Carlisle Evening Journal"

No. 13789 —8th W.Q. Registered at the G.P.O. as a Newspaper.   FRIDAY, MAY 24, 1957   Established 1798   PRICE TWOPENCE

VICKERS GREETS DEATH SENTENCE WITH A SHRUG

"No Room For Doubt," Says Judge

MANSLAUGHTER PLEA TO JURY FAILS

JOHN WILLSON VICKERS, 22-year-old Carlisle labourer, shrugged his shoulders as he was led down from the dock at Cumberland Assizes. yesterday after being sentenced to death.   A few minutes before the black cap was placed on the head of Mr. Justice Hinchcliffe, a jury of 10 men and two women had found Vickers guilty of the murder, on April 14, of elderly Carlisle shopkeeper Miss Jane Duckett, who was found dead in the basement of her Tait Street sweets and general grocery store.

The jury reached their verdict in the two-day trial after a retirement of one hour and seventeen minutes. Vickers, dressed in flannels, grey sports jacket, and with open-necked shirt, remained unmoved as he became the second man to be sentenced to death under the new Homicide Act.

He was told by the judge:

"You have been found guilty, by the verdict of the jury, of capital murder upon evidence which left no room for doubt. The sentence of the Court on you is that you suffer death in the manner authorised by law."

By its decision, the jury rejected a "manslaughter" plea advanced by Counsel for the defence Mr. D. Brabin, Q.C., who suggested that 72-year-old Miss Duckett moved her

as the 20th of March of this year.

This Act of Parliament classifies the types of murder, and it separates five types of murder from the rest. Of these five types ___

Mr. Justice Hinchcliffe leaving the Courts at Carlisle this week. In the background is Commander F. M. Fox, the High Sheriff.

Newspaper report of Vickers receiving the death sentence for capital murder in May 1957. Carlisle Journal

The enquiries very quickly led the police to suspect John Vickers, a single man from Penrith, who had been living at 10 Aglionby Street in Carlisle for about nine months. He was arrested at Penrith in the early hours of Wednesday 17 April. Glass and flakes of paint matching that from the broken window was found in the turn ups of Vickers' trousers and an imprint of a shoe on a piece of glass at the scene matched the pattern of the shoes he was wearing when he was arrested. Scratches to Vickers' face were further evidence that he was the guilty party. Vickers eventually admitted the break in but said he had no intention of hurting Jane. He had been on his way home from a dance and saw an opportunity to obtain some money so had broken the basement window of the shop and climbed in. He heard Jane coming down the stairs so tried to hide but she had seen him. Jane went for him with her arms upraised and that was how he had obtained the scratches. Vickers said he had hit her to defend himself and, thinking her only unconscious, had searched through the premises. Finding nothing of value he had left by the front door. In a rather ironic twist the police later found almost £900 hidden in a wardrobe.

Vickers stood at the Cumberland Assizes at Carlisle before Justice Hinchcliffe on Thursday 23 May 1957 with Jack Di V Nahum and DP Bailey acting for the prosecution and DJ Brabin and C Morris Jones for the defence. At the end of the two day trial the jury of ten men and two women found Vickers guilty and he was sentenced to death. He appealed against the death sentence on the grounds that he had acted in self defence against Jane's onslaught. His appeal was denied. Changes concerning the punishment for certain crimes had been made under the Homicide Act of 1957 that had come into force in March of that year. Murder in the furtherance of theft was a capital crime and could incur the death penalty. Although he had not actually stolen anything his intention had been robbery. Vickers received the dubious distinction of being the first man executed for the capital crime of murder under the new Act. He was hanged by James Billington on Tuesday 23 July 1957. It was later reported that he went to his end bravely and with resignation. A crowd of about seventy people stood on the green outside the gaol but under the new Act the custom of placing a notice outside the gaol to confirm the execution had taken place had been abolished.

At 9.14 am, Billington walked out of the gates which confirmed to those waiting it was all over. A general announcement was made from the Home Office at 10 am that justice had been served.

CHAPTER 36

The Jobber
1958

Frank Stokes was forty-four and a hotel porter. At the time of the following events he was of no fixed address and unemployed. On Monday 14 April he answered an advertisement for a jobbing gardener. The ad had been placed by Mrs Linda Violet Ash, a seventy-five-year-old widow, living at 41 Marlborough Avenue in Gosforth. That evening Sybil Tait, who rented a flat from Linda, returned home to find the inner door locked. She entered the house through the garage and found the elderly lady lying unconscious on the kitchen floor and covered in blood. The police and a doctor were called and Linda was rushed to the Newcastle Royal Infirmary where she died the following day. It was established that the cause of death was a fracture of the skull with the blows having been inflicted from behind. She had suffered three terrible wounds to the head, any one of which would have been severe enough to have killed the frail old lady. Linda's daughter searched through her mother's belongings but at that time could find nothing missing. The police were baffled, if not theft then where was a motive for this brutal killing. A hunt for the murderer was set in motion.

Neighbours had seen a stranger in the vicinity on that day. Ann Pickering, who lived in Marlborough Avenue, remembered a man asking for a number in the street and she had pointed him in the direction of Linda's house. Sybil Tait stated that on that day she had answered the door to a man who said he had come in answer to the advertisement for a gardener. Sybil went out leaving Linda and the man talking on the doorstep. Later that day John King, another man who was looking for a job, called twice at the house but received no answer. By that time Linda had already been attacked.

The house at Marlborough Avenue in Gosforth where Frank Stokes battered Linda Ash to death in 1938. Author's collection

Although the police spoke to five people who had seen the stranger in the vicinity, he was not to be found. If it was not for what happened a few days later, the murderer may never have been caught. On Friday 25 April, a man walked into Cannon Row Police Station in London and told Police Sergeant Michael Mather that he had killed a woman in Gosforth by hitting her on the head with a hammer. The man was Frank Stokes. Because the case had been widely publicised in the press in great detail, the police had to be very sure that Stokes really was their man so he was asked questions about the interior of the house where the crime was committed. As a matter of course, Stokes was searched at the police station. On his person a woman's purse was found.

The story Stokes gave was that he had gone to Newcastle and, after seeing the advertisement for a gardener, had taken a bus to Gosforth. After asking directions he went to the house for an interview. There were two women at the door, the younger one, who was Sybil, did not seem to like him very much but she left. Mrs Ash stood and spoke to him on the doorstep for a few minutes. She had then said she was nervous at inviting strangers into her house but asked him in anyway. He told Mrs Ash that he would work for 4s (20p) an hour. At first she seemed to agree but then changed her mind and said she would only pay 3s 6d (18p) an hour. Stokes said he became angry and smashed the lady's head in with a hammer. He said that he had not stolen any property from the premises except for the key with which he had locked the front door. If Stokes had not stolen anything, even though he had committed murder, this would not be a capital crime and imprisonment would be the maximum punishment the law would allow.

Linda's daughter would have been, understandably, upset when she first searched the house to see if anything was missing. On looking a second time she discovered that a purse that would have contained some notes could not be found. The purse found on Stokes resembled the description of the one that was missing from Linda's house but was of such a common type the daughter could not positively identify it as having belonged to her mother. Stokes' explanation to his possession of the purse was that he had answered an advertisement for a gardener at Ewell in Surrey and had stolen it from there. Why Stokes gave himself up for the murder is not known. Perhaps it was because he could not stand the guilt or because his description had been so widely circulated he thought he would be caught. He may have known the law and perhaps thought if theft could not be proved at the very worst he would spend a considerable number of years in prison.

His two day trial began on Monday, 21 July at Leeds Assizes before Justice Edmund Davies with Bernard Gillis and Rawdon Smith for the prosecution and G Waller and W Steer for the defence. The jury had to decide whether Stokes had gone to Linda's house with the intention of theft and whether he had carried out his intention. Stokes' plea was guilty of murder but not capital murder. The prosecution pointed out that, by his own admission, Stokes was a thief.

Because of the evidence and his confession there was no doubt that Stokes had committed the murder but the severity of his punishment would rest on what the jury believed was his motive for the crime. Although it was neither proved nor disproved that the purse had been taken from Linda's house a verdict of guilty of murder in the furtherance of theft was brought which, under the present law, brought with it sentence of death. The Criminal Court of Appeal denied a reprieve and Stokes was hanged on Wednesday 3 September 1958.

Fifteen women and one man were outside Durham Gaol waiting for the execution, scheduled for 9 am, to take place. The women were mainly off-duty cleaners from nearby Shire Hall. The man was a colliery engineer and a friend of Mrs Ash's family. He said he was waiting for the notice saying the execution had been carried out to be posted outside on the prison gates. He waited in vain as, unbeknown to him, the practice had been discontinued the previous year.

The End of the Rope, 1958
At about 10 pm on the night of Wednesday 11 June 1958 the badly beaten body of Martha Annie Dodd was discovered at her home at 4a Victoria Road in Darlington. The eighty-three-year-old widow had suffered a ferocious attack with no less than nineteen separate blows inflicted on her body with a hammer. As often happens with elderly people who live on their own, especially if they appear a little eccentric, there are often whispers about large sums of money that they are meant to have hoarded. It was rumoured that Mrs Dodd had the sum of £200 on her premises. The actual sum that the perpetrator of the attack had found was a mere £4.

On the police making initial enquiries they very quickly had a man in mind that they wished to interview and began a search for twenty-year-old Private Brian Chandler. Chandler was from Talbot Road in Middlesbrough and was stationed at the RAMC Catterick Camp Hospital. He had left his camp on Sunday 8 June and made his way to Darlington. On the night the murder had taken place Chandler, along with a friend, Marion Munro, had stayed at the house of Mr and Mrs Hill. The following morning Mr Hill heard that the police were looking for Chandler and advised him to go to the police station. At the initial police interview Chandler denied all knowledge of the crime but then changed his story and admitted that he had killed the old lady but not intentionally. Chandler told the police that he needed money so had offered to do some gardening for Martha. An argument took place over the 3s (15p) an hour she had offered to pay him. At the time Chandler was holding a bucket containing a hammer that Martha had handed to him. Martha had snatched the hammer and used it to attack him so he had hit back in self defence.

Chandler was arrested and stood trial before Justice Ashworth at Durham on Monday 27 October. His defence counsel, Stanley Price, had a difficult task as Chandler changed his story once again. He was now saying that he had planned to rob the old lady but had intended no violence. He and Munro had gone to the house on the pretence of looking for work and Martha had asked him to dig her garden. Chandler said that he had gone to retrieve a rake that she had loaned to the hotel next door. When he returned Munro had a hammer and was standing over Martha who was on the floor moaning. Munro had said to him that the old lady was not dead.

The case put forward by the prosecution headed by Rudolph Lyons was that Chandler had plotted with Marion Smith Munro, who was eighteen and from Hercules Road in Darlington, and Pauline Blair, who was seventeen from Chandos Street in Darlington, to carry out a robbery as they were in need of money. Munro had once worked for Martha and on telling her co-conspirators about her they decided that she was the perfect target. On Tuesday 10 June the three friends visited Martha telling her they were looking for work. Martha told them to return the following day and she might find something for them. Whilst at the house Chandler stole a bicycle but did not manage to find a buyer for it. He decided to return the following day to find and steal Martha's rumoured hoard of cash.

Munro and Blair both testified and admitted to plotting the robbery but denied any involvement in the murder. Munro stated that when Chandler said he was going to return to Martha's house to steal she had pointed out that the old lady would recognise them. Chandler had replied that if that was the case he would kill Martha. On the 11 June, Munro and Chandler parted company and met up again at about 3.30 pm along with another woman and a man. Chandler had some money and Munro asked where it had come from. Chandler casually said that he had killed a woman to get it. The man

The law courts at Carlisle where Brian Chandler was found guilty of the murder of Martha Dodds in 1958. Author's collection

and the woman noticed that there was a stain on Chandler's trousers which looked like blood.

When all the evidence had been heard the jury had to try and unravel the truth from the lies. They were out for about an hour and a half and returned with a verdict of guilty. They came to the conclusion that Chandler had told too many lies and that it was he, and he alone that had carried out the murder in the furtherance of theft. Under the Homicide Act of 1957 this was a capital crime and incurred the death penalty.

Chandler lodged an appeal but it was denied and he was hanged on Wednesday 17 December 1958 by Robert Stewart assisted by Thomas Cunliffe. This was to be the last time at Durham that the gallows and rope were to be put in place to send a person to their death.

Sources

Books
Diary of an Executioner, John Ellis
Executioner: Pierrepoint, Albert Pierrepoint, 1974
My Experiences as an Executioner, James Berry, 1892
The Hangman's Tale, Syd Dernley (with David Newman), 1989
The History and Antiquities of Darlington, Longstaffe, 1854

Newspapers
Carlisle Journal
Durham Advertiser
Durham Chronicle
Cumberland Evening News
Cumberland News
Newcastle Evening Chronicle
Northern Daily Mail
North Eastern Daily Gazette
South Durham and Cleveland Mercury
Yorkshire Evening Post
Yorkshire Post & Leeds Mercury

Index

People